Druid History, Mysticism, Ritua

The history of the Druids has a
first interest was reading as a
Magician who was also a Drui

Then I learned they were the ancient priests of the
Celts and had a deep history in the British Isles. My
family is also from Scotland and Northern Ireland so it
makes me wonder if I have some Druidic ancestry too.

Recently I wrote a book about the Mythical people of
Ireland and it also included materials about the Tuatha
Da Dannan who in many mythical histories were also
forerunners of the Druids.

Druids were also well known for their mystical
prophecy and healing abilities. Being a student of the
Paranormal and Spiritual this also holds a serious
interest for me.

In this book we will go through my research on Druid
history, festivals, rituals, herbs, alphabets, magic, and
much more.

Some Druidic rituals and exercises are also included.
In fact Druidism seems to be the source of many
modern approaches to witchcraft and magic.

Druid History, Mysticism, Rituals, Magic, and Prophecy

Druid History, Mysticism, Rituals, Magic, and Prophecy

Copyright Page

Druid History, Mysticism, Rituals, Magic, and Prophecy

Druid History, Mysticism, Rituals, Magic, and Prophecy

Other books by Martin K. Ettington

Druid History, Mysticism, Rituals, Magic, and Prophecy

Stranger Than Science Stories and Facts

Survival
Survival of Humanity Throughout the Ages
33 Incredible True Survival Stories
The Importance of Fire in History and Mythology
How to Survive Anything: From the Wilderness to Man Made Disasters
Building and Stocking a Nuclear Shelter for less than $10,000
The Human Survival Five Books Bundle

Legendary Beings
Are Cryptozoological Animals Real or Imaginary?
Fire in History and Mythology
All About Dragons
Sea Serpents and Ocean Monsters
The Legendary Animals Five Books Bundle
The Mythical People of Ireland
Bigfoot Mysteries and Some Answers
About the Little People: Fairies, Elves, Dwarfs and Leprechauns

Ancient History
The Real Atlantis-In the Eye of the Sahara
Ancient & Prehistoric Civilizations
Ancient & Prehistoric Civilizations-Book Two
The History of Antediluvian Giants
The Antediluvian History of Earth
Ancient Underground Cities and Tunnels
Strange Objects Which Should Not Exist
More Out of Place Artifacts
Strange and Ancient Places in the USA
A Theory of Ancient Prehistory And Giant Aliens
The Destruction of Civilization About 10,500 B.C.
A Timeline of Intelligent Life on Earth
A 300 Million Year Old Civilization Existed on Earth

Aliens and Space
Aliens and Secret Technology
Aliens Are Already Among Us

Designing and Building Space Colonies
Humanity and the Universe
All About Moon Bases
All About Mars Journeys and Settlement
The Space and Aliens Six Books Bundle
A Theory of Ancient Prehistory and Giant Aliens
The Space Colonies and Space Structures Coloring Book
All About Asteroids
Spaceships, Past, Present, and Future
Astronauts, Cosmonauts, and Other Important Space Flyers
All About Mars Journeys and Settlement
Mining the Asteroid Belt

Time Travel and Dimensions
Real Time Travel Stories From a Psychic Engineer
The Real Nature of Time: An Analysis of Physics, Prophecy, and Time Travel Experiences
Stories of Parallel Dimensions
We Live in a Malleable Reality-and We Can Change It
The Time, Dimensions, and Quantum Mechanical Bundle
Alternate Dimensions & the Otherworld

Political and Social

The Empire of the United States: Forged By God's Spirit Through Man

Druid History, Mysticism, Rituals, Magic, and Prophecy

The Longevity Training Series

(A transcription of the online Multimedia Longevity Coaching Training Program)

The Personal Longevity Training Series-Book1-Long Lived Persons
The Personal Longevity Training Series-Book2-Your Soul's Purpose
The Personal Longevity Training Series-Book3-Enable Your Life Urge
The Personal Longevity Training Series-Book4-Your Spiritual Connection
The Personal Longevity Training Series-Book5-Having Love in Your Heart
The Personal Longevity Training Series-Book6-Energy Body Health
The Personal Longevity Training Series-Book7-The Science of Longevity
The Personal Longevity Training Series-Book8-Physical Body Health
The Personal Longevity Training Series-Book9-Avoiding Accidents
The Personal Longevity Training Series-Book10-Implementing These Principles

The Personal Longevity Training Series-Books One Thru Ten

These books are all available in digital and printed formats from my website and on Amazon, Barnes & Noble, Apple ITunes, and many other sites

My Books Website is: http://mkettingtonbooks.com

Druid History, Mysticism, Rituals, Magic, and Prophecy

Druid History, Mysticism, Rituals, Magic, and Prophecy

Table of Contents

Druid History, Mysticism, Rituals, Magic, and Prophecy

Druid History, Mysticism, Rituals, Magic, and Prophecy

1.0 Introduction

The history of the Druids has always fascinated me. My first interest was reading as a child about Merlin the Magician who was also a Druid.

Then I learned they were the ancient priests of the Celts and had a deep history in the British Isles. My family is also from Scotland and Northern Ireland so it makes me wonder if I have some Druidic ancestry too.

Recently I wrote a book about the Mythical people of Ireland and it also included materials about the Tuatha Da Dannan who in many mythical histories were also forerunners of the Druids.

Druids were also well known for their mystical prophecy and healing abilities. Being a student of the Paranormal and Spiritual this also holds a serious interest for me.

In this book we will go through my research on Druid history, festivals, rituals, herbs, alphabets, magic, and much more.

Some Druidic rituals and exercises are also included. In fact Druidism seems to be the source of many modern approaches to witchcraft and magic.

Druid History, Mysticism, Rituals, Magic, and Prophecy

2.0 Historical Perspectives of the Druids

In this chapter we will examine the history of the Druids from several perspectives including mythical, legends, modern druids, and more.

2.1 Who Were the Druids?

Druids occur in many mystical tales. In one, a Druid, Figol, threatened to bring fire to rage on his enemies and prevent the men and their steeds from going to the toilet! Their bodies would fill with urine! Of course, from our knowledge of the world today we know that this is impossible, but so many accounts of druids are riddled with mysticism, magic and possible exaggeration.

The origin of the word 'Druid'' is unclear, but the most popular view is that it comes from 'doire', an Irish-Gaelic word for oak tree (often a symbol of knowledge), also meaning 'wisdom'. Druids were concerned with the natural world and its powers, and considered trees sacred, particularly the oak.

Druid History, Mysticism, Rituals, Magic, and Prophecy

Druidism can be described as a shamanic religion, as it relied on a combination of contact with the spirit world and holistic medicines to treat (and sometimes cause) illnesses. They were said to have induced insanity in people and been accurate fortune tellers. Some of their knowledge of the earth and space may have come from megalithic times.

There is a lot of mystery shrouding the actual history of the Druids, as our knowledge is based on limited records. Druidism is thought to have been a part of Celtic and Gaulish culture in Europe, with the first classical reference to them in the 2nd century BC.

Their practices were similar to those of priests today, connecting the people with the gods, but their role was also varied and wide-ranging, acting as teachers, scientists, judges and philosophers. They were incredibly powerful and respected, able to banish people from society for breaking the sacred laws, and even able to come between two opposing armies and prevent warfare! They did not have to pay taxes or serve in battle. Druid women were also considered equal to men in many respects, unusual for an ancient community. They could take part in wars and even divorce their husbands!

One of the earliest accounts of Druids was written by Julius Caesar in 59-51 B.C. He wrote it in Gaul, where prestigious men were divided into Druids or nobles. It was from the Roman writers that historians have gained most of their knowledge of the Druids. Druids were polytheistic and had female gods and sacred figures, rather like the Greeks and Romans, but their nomadic, less civilized Druidic society gave the others a sense of superiority. This renders some of their accounts historically uncertain, as they may be tainted with exaggerated examples of Druidic practices.

Druidic human sacrifice was recorded but there is no definitive evidence to support this.

Within the Druid class, it is believed that there were subsections, all with colour-coded robes. The eldest Druid, or one deemed to be the most wise, was the Arch-druid, and would wear gold robes. The ordinary Druids would wear white and act as priests. The Sacrificers would fight and wear red. The blue Bards were artistic, and the new recruits to Druidism completed lesser tasks and were held in lesser esteem, wearing brown or black.

All aspects of Druidism were well structured and ordered; from the hierarchy of the Druid class, to their pattern of life that followed nature's cycles. They observed lunar, solar and seasonal cycles and worshipped according to these on 8 main holy days.

They would celebrate New Year on **Samhain**, the day that we refer to as Halloween (31st October). This was when the last harvest would take place and it was a day full of mysticism and spirituality because the living and the deceased were the closest to being revealed to each other than on any other day.

Yule was the winter solstice, a time when Druids would sit on mounds of earth, for example at New Grange in Ireland, throughout the night, waiting for sunrise, when they would be reborn!

Imbolc (2nd February) involved using sheep's milk by way of celebrating motherhood. **Ostara** was the spring equinox, and **Beltane** took place on 30th April as a festival of fertility. **Litha** was the summer solstice, a time when they believed that the 'holly king' took over from the 'oak king' of Yule. **Lughnasa** was the first harvest on 2nd August and **Mabon** was the autumnal equinox. Then the cycle of holy days would repeat itself again, reflecting the cycles of nature, planets and indeed life itself, as the Druids believed in reincarnation. They also believed that sins committed in a previous life could be made up for in the next.

Druid History, Mysticism, Rituals, Magic, and Prophecy

Their places of worship ('Temples of the Druids') were quiet, secluded areas, like clearings in woods and forests, and stone circles. Probably the most famous stone circle in Britain is Stonehenge, an ancient megalithic monument dating back to about 2400 B.C. Most people's first thoughts about the Druids might be of them congregating around Stonehenge and casting magical incantations.

There is indeed thought that this was a place of worship for them, as it still is today for pagans and other neo-druids. There is disagreement though, about whether the Druids built Stonehenge or not. It is not clear exactly when the Druids came to Britain, but it is likely that they actually arrived after Stonehenge was built.

The Isle of Ynys Mon, Anglesey, and Wistman's Wood in Dartmoor are both believed to be Druidic sites. Indeed, Anglesey was supposedly a place where Druids were taught. It took about 20 years to learn the lore, as it was complex and had to be learnt off by heart as they rarely used a written language. This is one reason why we know so little about them. The Gaul's had a limited written language, involving Greek characters, and then with Caesar's rule this became Latin and old records were lost. Some legends must also be treated with caution as they may have even been altered by subsequent Christian influence or exaggeration.

In the 1st century AD, Druids were facing oppression from the Romans. Indeed, Tiberius banned Druidism because of the supposed human sacrifices. After this, in 2nd century, Druidism appeared to end. There are a couple of theories to try and explain this. The first is that, as with many ancient societies, disease, famine or warfare could have wiped them out. The second implicates the arrival of Christianity in the decline. Might they have been converted? In the 1700s though, a Druid revival occurred in England and Wales. The famous William Blake (an Arch-druid) even took part in this.

Druid History, Mysticism, Rituals, Magic, and Prophecy

Some religions today, like Christianity and Wicca have been influenced by Druidry. The number three was considered greatly significant in Druid lore, and also by these religions. For example, the Triscale was a symbol involving 3 lines coming together to form a circle. Circles were key to many Druid beliefs; the circle of life, the seasons, light and darkness.

It would surprise many to learn that Winston Churchill was supposed to be a Druid!

Druid History, Mysticism, Rituals, Magic, and Prophecy

2.2 The Tuatha Da Dannan Who Came Before

The Tuatha De Danann are the ancient beings of Ireland who legend says are the forefathers of Druids, Elves, and Leprechauns.

The Legend of the Tuatha De Danann

The Tuatha Dé Danann were descended from Nemed, leader of a previous wave of inhabitants of Ireland. They came from four cities to the north of Ireland—Falias, Gorias, Murias and Finias—where they taught their skills in the sciences, including architecture, the arts, and magic, including necromancy. According to Lebor Gabála Érenn, they came to Ireland "in dark clouds" and "landed on the mountains of [the] Conmaicne Rein in Connachta", otherwise Sliabh an Iarainn, "and they brought a darkness over the sun for three days and three nights". They immediately burnt the ships "so that they should not think of retreating to them, and the smoke and the mist that came from the vessels filled the neighbouring land and air.

Therefore it was conceived that they had arrived in clouds of mist".

A poem in the Lebor Gabála Érenn says of their arrival:

It is God who suffered them, though He restrained them
they landed with horror, with lofty deed,
in their cloud of mighty combat of spectres,
upon a mountain of Conmaicne of Connacht.

Without distinction to discerning Ireland,
Without ships, a ruthless course
the truth was not known beneath the sky of stars,
whether they were of heaven or of earth.

According to Tuan:

From them are the Tuatha Dé and Andé, whose origin the learned do not know, but that it seems likely to them that they came from heaven, on account of their intelligence and for the excellence of their knowledge.

Led by king Nuada, they fought the First Battle of Magh Tuireadh on the west coast, in which they defeated and displaced the native Fir Bolg, who then inhabited Ireland.

In the battle, Nuada lost an arm to their champion, Sreng. Since Nuada was no longer "unblemished", he could not continue as king and was replaced by the half-Fomorian Bres, who turned out to be a tyrant. The physician Dian Cecht replaced Nuada's arm with a working silver one and he was reinstated as king. However, Dian Cecht's son Miach was dissatisfied with the replacement so he recited the spell, "ault fri halt dí & féith fri féth" (joint to joint of it and sinew to sinew), which caused flesh to grow over the silver prosthesis over the course of nine days and nights.

However, in a fit of jealous rage Dian Cecht slew his own son. Because of Nuada's restoration as the leader, Bres complained to his family and his father, Elatha, who sent him to seek assistance from Balor, king of the Fomorians.

The Tuatha Dé Danann then fought the Second Battle of Magh Tuireadh against the Fomorians. Nuada was killed by the Fomorian king Balor's poisonous eye, but Balor was killed by Lugh, champion of the Tuatha Dé, and who then took over as king.

A third battle was fought against a subsequent wave of invaders, the Milesians, from the northwest of the Iberian Peninsula (present-day Galicia and Northern Portugal), descendants of Míl Espáine (who are thought to represent the Goidelic Celts). The Milesians encountered three Tuatha Dé Danann goddesses, Ériu, Banba and Fodla, who asked that the island be named after them; Ériu is the origin of the modern name Éire, and Banba and Fodla are still sometimes used as poetic names for Ireland.

Their three husbands, Mac Cuill, Mac Cecht and Mac Gréine, were kings of the Tuatha Dé Danann at that time, and asked for a truce of three days, during which the Milesians would lie at anchor nine waves' distance from the shore. The Milesians complied, but the Tuatha Dé Danann created a magical storm in an attempt to drive them away. The Milesian poet Amergin calmed the sea with his verse, then his people landed and defeated the Tuatha Dé Danann at Tailtiu. When Amergin was called upon to divide the land between the Tuatha Dé Danann and his own people, he cleverly allotted the portion above ground to the Milesians and the portion underground to the Tuatha Dé Danann. The Tuatha Dé Danann were led underground into the Sidhe mounds by Manannán mac Lir and Tir na nOg onto a flowery plain/plain of honey attested to in the Voyage of Bran.

Where They Came From

The Tuath(a) Dé Danann also known by the earlier name Tuath Dé ("tribe of the gods"), are a supernatural race in Irish mythology. They are thought to represent the main deities of pre-Christian Gaelic Ireland. The Tuatha Dé Danann constitute a pantheon whose attributes appeared in a number of forms throughout the Celtic world.

The Tuath Dé dwell in the Otherworld but interact with humans and the human world. They are associated with ancient passage tombs, such as Brú na Bóinne, which were seen as portals to the Otherworld. Their traditional rivals are the Fomorians (Fomoire), who seem to represent the harmful or destructive powers of nature, and who the Tuath Dé defeat in the Battle of Mag Tuired. Each member of the Tuath Dé has associations with a particular feature of life or nature, but many appear to have more than one association. Many also have bynames, some representing different aspects of the deity and others being regional names or epithets.

Much of Irish mythology was recorded by Christian monks, who modified it to an extent. They often depicted the Tuath Dé as kings, queens and heroes of the distant past who had supernatural powers. Other times they were explained as fallen angels who were neither good nor evil. However, some medieval writers acknowledged that they were gods.

They also appear in tales set centuries apart, showing them to be immortal. Prominent members of the Tuath Dé include The Dagda, who seems to have been a chief god; The Morrígan; Lugh; Nuada; Aengus; Brigid; Manannán, a god of the sea; Dian Cecht, a god of healing; and Goibniu, a god of metalworking and blacksmithing as well as one of the Trí Dé Dána ("three gods of craftsmanship"). They have parallels in the pantheons of other Celtic peoples: for example Lugh is cognate with the pan-Celtic god Lugus, Nuada with the British god Nodens, Brigid with Brigantia; Tuirenn with Taranis; Ogma with Ogmios; and the Badb with Cathubodua.

The Tuath Dé eventually became the Aos Sí or "fairies" of later folklore.

Druid History, Mysticism, Rituals, Magic, and Prophecy

2.3 Druids in Classical History

A druid was a member of the high-ranking class in ancient
Celtic cultures. Druids were religious leaders as well as
legal authorities, adjudicators, lorekeepers, medical
professionals and political advisors. Druids left no written
accounts. While they were reported to have been literate,
they are believed to have been prevented by doctrine from
recording their knowledge in written form. Their beliefs and
practices are attested in some detail by their
contemporaries from other cultures, such as the Romans
and the Greeks.

The earliest known references to the druids date to the 4th
century BCE. The oldest detailed description comes from
Julius Caesar's Commentarii de Bello Gallico (50s BC).
They were described by other Roman writers such as
Cicero, Tacitus, and Pliny the Elder. Following the Roman
invasion of Gaul, the druid orders were suppressed by the
Roman government under the 1st-century CE emperors
Tiberius and Claudius, and had disappeared from the
written record by the 2nd century.

In about 750 CE, the word druid appears in a poem by
Blathmac, who wrote about Jesus, saying that he was
"better than a prophet, more knowledgeable than every
druid, a king who was a bishop and a complete sage."] The
druids appear in some of the medieval tales from
Christianized Ireland like "Táin Bó Cúailnge", where they
are largely portrayed as sorcerers who opposed the
coming of Christianity. In the wake of the Celtic revival
during the 18th and 19th centuries, fraternal and neopagan
groups were founded based on ideas about the ancient
druids, a movement known as Neo-Druidism. Many
popular notions about druids, based on misconceptions of

18th-century scholars, have been largely superseded by more recent study.

2.4 Druidism in England

Our knowledge of Druidism is often full of misconceptions, here's everything you need to know about the history of Druidism and Druids in Britain:

Although it has become commonplace to associate England's most famous stone circle, Stonehenge, with the mysterious ancient order known as the Druids, in truth, the two have little or no historical connection. This fallacy is just one of many misconceptions about Druids that has carried over into the modern age.

Druidism, in fact, traces its origins to ancient Wales, where the order began long before the advent of written history. Druids were the priests of the early Celtic religion, on the top rung of the three-tiered Celtic society consisting of serfs, warriors, and learned men. But in addition to their religious function, Druids also performed the roles of judge, doctor, and scholar. They were educated through a long and grueling process of rote memorization. Druidic law forbade its followers to write down any of the religious teachings, a rule that has unfortunately prevented us from having firsthand knowledge of their Celtic religion.

What historical records we do have of the Druids come to us from non-objective sources: Posidonius, a Greek writer who supposedly visited Gaul in the second century BC; Julius Caesar, who recorded his observations about the Druids in his account of the Gallic War, written after the Roman invasion of the British Isles; and the Roman writer Tacitus whose Annals of Imperial Rome and Germanica were written after the consolidation of Britain. In these records, the writers all remark upon the Druids' extensive knowledge, particularly in the fields of mathematics, astronomy, and physics.

The religious practices of Druids

But in addition to their learning, early historians also took note of what they considered to be the Druids' barbaric religious practices. In particular, they were appalled by the use of human sacrifice. The Romans reported that victims were tied to wicker effigies and burned alive, a report substantiated by archaeological remains. Further evidence has been found of 'triple deaths' where a victim was simultaneously stoned, drowned, and impaled on a spear.

Celtic religion did involve elements of ritual sacrifice, but Druids (and Celts in general) did not conceive of death the way in which we do today.

As Caesar comments: 'The cardinal doctrine which they seek to teach is that souls do not die, but after death pass from one to another. . . the fear of death is cast aside." Often, sacrifice involved a spiritual trade of sorts, sacrificing a less prominent member of society so that someone more important might survive.

Caesar wrote: "The whole nation of the Gauls is greatly devoted to ritual observances and for that reason those who are smitten with the more grievous maladies and who are engaged in the peril of battle either sacrifice human victims or vow to do so, employing the druids as ministers for such sacrifice. They believe in effect, that, unless a man's life be paid, the majesty of the immortal gods may not be appeased."

These accounts were, no doubt, colored by the Romans' personal biases. Caesar, in particular, was trying to garner support for his campaign from his audience at home, a task made easier by painting a barbaric picture of the

Druids. Barbaric, to a Roman audience who flocked to see equally gruesome deaths at the hands of the gladiators.

Nevertheless, both Roman and Greek historians did record the Druids' highly organized legal and educational systems and seemed to revere their mathematical and scientific knowledge. Both sources considered the Druids to be 'noble savages', a highly learned but religiously primitive people who worshipped a pantheon of gods.

The Massacre of the Druids

After Emperor Claudius declared Druidic practices illegal in AD 54, the Druids' future in Roman Britain became increasingly uncertain. In AD 61, the Romans planned a massacre of the defiant Druids at Anglesey, the center of their culture, and their last stronghold in consolidated Britain. As the Roman soldiers waited for the tide to recede so they could cross the Menai strait that separates Anglesey from the mainland, the Druids held their position by lining up along the opposite shore and, as Tacitus reports in his Annals, 'raising their hands to heaven and screaming dreadful curses.' But curses were not enough. The Roman soldiers crossed the strait and conquered the island, destroying both the Druids and the sacred groves of their religion.

Following this defeat, the Druidic culture never again flourished as it did in these early days. Pockets of it persisted in Ireland, however, and forward-thinking monks in both Ireland and Wales preserved some Druidic traditions. Much of what was known about Druids continued to exist solely in the oral tradition until the Medieval period when it was transcribed and edited by Christian monks. Although these records come filtered through a biased source, these manuscripts have passed on much of what we know today about the Druids of ancient Britain. In Ireland, these myths exist in four chief cycles: the Ulster Cycle, the Fionn Cycle, the Invasion Races, and the Cycle of Kings. In Wales, the primary source of Druidic information, and indeed the very cornerstone of Welsh literary tradition, exists in The Mabinogion, a collection of myths and tales transcribed in the 11th century.

The interest in Druidism

In the early 18th century, interest in Druidism underwent a revival, primarily as a result of the less-than-noble efforts of one man, Edward Williams, or, Iolo Morganwyg as he was known, who claimed to have discovered an ancient Welsh book of Druidic knowledge. This book, called The Barddas was later revealed to be a forgery. Morgannwg made up most of what was contained within, including the ceremony of Gorsedd Beirdd Ynys Prydain, or, The Assembly of Bards on the Isle of Britain. Morgannwg held the first Gorsedd ceremony in 1792 on London's Primrose Hill.

A similar type of ceremony, incorporating elements of ancient Druidic ritual, had been taking place in Wales for hundreds of years prior to Morganwyg's event. The Eisteddfod, an annual celebratory gathering of Welsh bards, dates back to the 15th century. By the 1700s, however, interest was waning and enthusiasm for the event was low. In 1858, however, Morganwyg's Gorsedd ceremonies, although wholly fictitious, were incorporated into the Eisteddfod, and gave it a new life.

It was during this period of Romantic Revival that most of the misconceptions about Druidism took root. The most common, linking Druids with Stonehenge, is clearly a fallacy. Recent archaeological findings date Stonehenge to more than 2,000 years before the rise of Druidism. Although Druids did use stone circles and astronomical calculations in their spiritual practices, no such monuments of their making have survived.

Modern-day Druids

Modern-day Druids, however, have latched on to the connection, and often hold solstice celebrations at Stonehenge. (Unlike their ancient predecessors, no human sacrifice is involved.) Indeed, Druidism is alive and well today and enjoying a late 20th-century revival of sorts. The Eisteddfod still celebrated annually in Wales, is held during the first week of August each year. Although the modern ceremony has veered more towards the cultural, rather than religious, celebration, the Eisteddfod remains true to its Druidic roots.

But just as the sacrificial rituals of the ancient Druids created controversy in ancient times, so today modern Druids find themselves at the center of the debate. This controversy comes to a head around the 21st of June each year when modern Druids converge upon what is undoubtedly one of the most-visited tourist attractions in all of Britain to commemorate the summer solstice. English Heritage and The National Trust, who jointly manage the property are usually less than welcoming to these annual uninvited guests. Stonehenge, which stood before even the original Druids may have gathered among its mysterious stones somehow puts the controversy into perspective."

Druid History, Mysticism, Rituals, Magic, and Prophecy

2.5 Merlin the Druid Magician

The famous Merlin the Magician was also the most famous Druid.

The Legendary Origins of Merlin the Magician

Most people today have heard of Merlin the Magician, as his name has been popularized over the centuries and his story has been dramatized in numerous novels, films, and television programs. The powerful wizard is depicted with many magical powers, including the power of shapeshifting, and is well-known in mythology as a tutor and mentor to the legendary King Arthur, ultimately guiding him towards becoming the king of Camelot. While these general tales are well-known, Merlin's initial appearances were only somewhat linked to Arthur. It took many decades of adaptations before Merlin became the wizard of Arthurian legend he is known as today.

Merlin the wizard

<u>Merlin and Ambrosius</u>

It is common belief that Merlin was created as a figure for **Arthurian legend.** While Merlin the Wizard was a very prominent character in the stories of Camelot, that is not where he originated. Writer Geoffrey of Monmouth is credited with creating Merlin in his 1136 AD work, *Historia Regum Britanniae* – The History of Kings of Britain. While a large portion of *Historia Regum Britanniae* is a historical account of the former kings of Britain, Merlin was included as a fictional character (although it is likely that Geoffrey intended for readers to believe he was a figure extracted from long-lost ancient texts). Merlin was paradoxical, as he was both the son of the **devil** and the servant of God.

Merlin was created as a combination of several historical and legendary figures. Geoffrey combined stories of North Brythonic **prophet** and madman, Myrddin Wyllt, and Romano-British war leader, **Ambrosius Aurelianus** , to create Merlin Ambrosius. Ambrosius was a figure in Nennius' *Historia Brittonum*. In *Historia Brittonum*, British king Vortigern wished to erect a tower, but each time he tried, it would collapse before completion. He was told that to prevent this, he would have to first sprinkle the ground beneath the tower with the blood of a child who was born without a father. Ambrosius was thought to have been born without a father, so he was brought before Vortigern. Ambrosius explained to Vortigern that the tower could not be supported upon the foundation because two battling dragons lived beneath, representing the **Saxons** and the Britons. Ambrosius convinced Vortigern that the tower would only stand with Ambrosius as a leader, and Vortigern gave Ambrosius the tower, which was also the kingdom. Geoffrey retold this story with Merlin as the child born without a father, although he retained the character of Ambrosius.

Illumination of a 15th century manuscript of Historia Regum Britanniae showing king of the Britons Vortigern and Ambros watching the fight between two dragons.

In Geoffrey's version of the story, he included a long section containing Merlin's prophecies, along with two other stories, which led to the inclusion of Merlin into **Arthurian legend** . These include the tale of Merlin creating Stonehenge as the burial location for Ambrosius, and the story of Uther Pendragon sneaking into Tintagel where he fathered Arthur with Igraine, his enemy's wife. This was the extent of Geoffrey's tales of Merlin. Geoffrey does not include any stories of Merlin acting as a tutor to Arthur, which is how Merlin is most well-known today. Geoffery's character of Merlin quickly became popular, particularly in Wales, and from there the tales were adapted, eventually leading to Merlin's role as Arthur's tutor.

A giant helps Merlin build Stonehenge. From a manuscript of the Roman de Brut by Wace.

Merlin – The Poem

Many years after Geoffrey's *Historia Regum Britanniae* , Robert de Boron composed a poem called *Merlin*. Boron's Merlin has the same origins as Geoffrey's creation, but Boron placed special emphasis on Merlin's shapeshifting powers, connection to the **Holy Grail**, and his **jokester** personality. Boron also introduced Blaise, Merlin's master.

Boron's poem was eventually re-written in prose as *Estoire de Merlin,* which also places much focus upon Merlin's shapeshifting. Over the years, Merlin was interspersed through the tales of Arthurian legend. Some writings placed much focus upon Merlin as Arthur's mentor, while others did not mention Merlin at all. In some tales Merlin was viewed as an evil figure who did no good in his life, while in others he was viewed favorably as Arthur's teacher and mentor.

Merlin's Love and Death

Eventually, from the various tales emerged Merlin's downfall, at the hands of Niviane (Vivien), the king of Northumberland's daughter. Arthur convinces Niviane to stay in his castle, under Merlin's encouragement. Merlin falls in love with Niviane. However, Niviane fears Merlin will use his magical powers to take advantage of her. She swears that she will never fall in love with him, unless he teaches her all of the magic he knows. Merlin agrees. Merlin and Niviane depart to return to Northumberland, when they are called back to assist King Arthur. As they are returning, they stop to stay in a stone chamber, where two lovers once died and were buried together. When Merlin falls asleep, Niviane places him under a spell, and traps him within the stone tomb, where he dies. Merlin had never realized that his desire for Niviane, and his willingness to teach her his magical ways eventually led to his untimely death.

Merlin the Wizard's Legacy

In 2019, fragments of a rare manuscript published in the 1500s were found in the University of Bristol's special collections library **detailing** "subtle but significant differences from the traditional story" of Merlin the magician. For example, the deaths of some characters in the stories are different from more traditional accounts and there are more detailed descriptions of key events such as battles.

3.0 Druid Festivals

There are four solar and four lunar festivals – creating thereby a balanced scheme of interlocking masculine and feminine observances. The solar observances are the ones that most people associate with modern-day Druids – particularly the Summer Solstice ceremonies at Stonehenge.

At the Solstices, the Sun is revered at the point of its apparent death at midwinter – and of its maximum power at the noon of the year when the days are longest. At the Equinoxes, day and night are balanced. At the Spring Equinox, the power of the sun is on the increase, and we celebrate the time of sowing and of preparation for the gifts of Summer. At the Autumnal Equinox, although day and night are of equal duration, the power of the sun is on the wane, and we give thanks for the gifts of the harvest and prepare for the darkness of Winter.

These four festivals are astronomical observances, and we can be sure our ancestors marked them with ritual because many of the stone circles are oriented to their points of sunrise or sunset. By the time the circles were built, our ancestors had become a pastoral people, and times of sowing and reaping were vital to them.

But as well as these four astronomical, solar festivals, there exist four times in the year which were and are also considered sacred. These were the times which were more associated with the livestock cycle, rather than the farming cycle.

October 31st – November 2nd: Samhuinn

Looking at the complete cycle, we shall begin at Samhuinn – a time which marked traditionally the ending and the beginning of the Celtic Year.

Samhuinn, from October 31st to November 2nd, was a time of no-time. Celtic society, like all early societies, was highly structured and organized – everyone knew their place. But to allow that order to be psychologically comfortable, the Celts knew that there had to be a time when order and structure were abolished – when chaos could reign. And Samhuinn was such a time. Time was abolished for the three days of this festival, and people did crazy things – men dressed as women and women as men. Farmers' gates were unhinged and left in ditches, peoples' horses were moved to different fields, and children would knock on neighbors' doors for food and treats in a way that we still find today, in a watered-down way, in the custom of trick-or-treating on Hallowe'en.

But behind this apparent lunacy, lay a deeper meaning. The Druids knew that these three days had a special quality about them. The veil between this world and the World of the Ancestors was drawn aside on these nights, and for those who were prepared, journeys could be made in safety to the 'other side'. The Druid rites, therefore, were concerned with making contact with the spirits of the departed, who were seen as sources of guidance and inspiration rather than as sources of dread.

The dark moon, the time when no moon can be seen in the sky, was the phase of the moon which ruled this time, because it represents a time in which our mortal sight needs to be obscured in order for us to see into the other worlds.

The dead are honored and feasted, not as the dead, but as the living spirits of loved ones and of guardians who hold the root-wisdom of the tribe. With the coming of Christianity, this festival was turned into All Hallows [commonly referred to as Hallowe'en on October 31st], All Saints [November 1st] and All Souls [November 2nd]. Here we can see most clearly the way in which Christianity built on the pagan foundations it found rooted in these isles. Not only does the purpose of the festival match with the earlier one, but even the unusual length of the festival is the same.

21st December – Winter Solstice

Next in the cycle is the time of the Winter Solstice, called in the Druid Tradition Alban Arthan [the Light of Arthur]. This is the time of death and rebirth. The sun appears to be abandoning us completely as the longest night comes to us. Linking our own inner journey to the yearly cycle, the words of the Druid ceremony ask "Cast away, O wo/man whatever impedes the appearance of light." In darkness we throw on to the ground the scraps of material we have been carrying that signify those things which have been holding us back, and one lamp is lit from a flint and raised up on the Druid's crook in the East. The year is reborn and a new cycle begins, which will reach its peak at the time of the Midsummer Solstice, before returning again to the place of death-and-birth.

Although the Bible indicates that Jesus was born in the Spring, it is no accident that the early Church chose to move his official birthday to the time of the Midwinter Solstice – for it is indeed a time when the Light enters the darkness of the World, and we see again the building of Christianity on the foundations of earlier belief.

In a Christian culture we really only have one marker for the year, and that is Christmas. Easter and Harvest-time used to be significant, but can hardly be considered so now, when only a fraction of the British population attend Church regularly.

February 1st – Imbolc

Druidry has eight markers, which means that every six weeks or so, we have the opportunity to step out of the humdrum of daily life, to honor the conjunction of Place and Time.

The next Festival occurs on February 2nd, or the eve of February 1st. It is called Imbolc in the Druid tradition, or sometimes Oimelc. Although we would think of Imbolc as being in the midst of Winter, it represents in fact the first of a trio of Spring celebrations, since it is the time of the first appearance of the snowdrop, and of the melting of the snows and the clearing of the debris of Winter. It is a time when we sense the first glimmer of Spring, and when the lambs are born. In the Druid tradition it is a gentle, beautiful festival in which the Mother Goddess is honored with eight candles rising out of the water at the center of the ceremonial circle.

The Goddess that ruled Samhuinn was the Cailleach, the Grey Hag, the Mountain Mother, the Dark Woman of Knowledge. But by Imbolc the Goddess has become Brighid, the Goddess of poets, healers and midwives.

And so we often use Imbolc as a time for an Eisteddfod dedicated to poetry and song praising the Goddess in her many forms. The Christian development of this festival is Candlemas – the time of the Presentation of Christ in the Temple. For years successive Popes had tried to stop parades of lit candles in the streets of Rome at this time, until seeing that it was impossible to put a stop to this pagan custom, they suggested that everyone enter the churches so that the priests could bless the candles.

March 21st – Spring Equinox

Time moves on, and in a short while we come to the Spring Equinox – the time of equality of day and night, when the forces of the light are on the increase. At the center of the trio of Spring Festas, Alban Eilir [the Light of the Earth] marks the more recognizable beginnings of Spring, when the flowers are beginning to appear and when the sowing begins in earnest.

As the point of psychological development in our lives it marks the time of late childhood to, say, 14 years – Imbolc marking the time of early childhood [say to 7yrs].

We are in the Spring of our lives – the seeds that are planted in our childhood time of Imbolc and Alban Eilir will flower from the Beltane time of adolescence onwards as capacities and powers that will help us to negotiate our lives with skill and accomplishment.

May 1st – Beltane

Beltane, on May 1st, marks the time of our adolescence and early wo/manhood. Spring is in full bloom, and twin fires would be lit at this time, through which would be passed the cattle after their long winter confinement, or over which those hoping for a child or good fortune would jump.

We see traces of the Beltane celebrations on May Day, when dancing round the maypole celebrates the fertility of the land and creates an echo of the ritual circle dances that must have been enacted in stone circles throughout the country.

June 21st – Summer Solstice

We have reached the time of the Summer Solstice, Alban Hefin, The Light of the Shore, by June 21st or 22nd [the dates for each of the solar festivals vary each year since the events are astronomical not man-made, like our calendar]. Light is at its maximum, and this is the time of the longest day. It is at this time that the Druids hold their most complex ceremony. Starting at midnight on the eve of the Solstice, a vigil is held through the night – seated around the Solstice fire. The night is over in a matter of hours, and as light breaks, the Dawn Ceremony marks the time of the sun's rising on this his most powerful day. At noon a further ceremony is held.

August 1st – Lughnasadh

Six weeks later we come to the time of Lughnasadh on August 1st, which marks the beginning of harvest time.

The hay would have been gathered in, and the time for reaping the wheat and barley was due. It was a time of gathering together, of contests and games and of marriages. The marriages contracted at this time could be annulled at the same time the following year – offering the couple a sensible 'trial period'. In some areas a flaming wheel was sent rolling down the hillside at this time to symbolize the descent of the year towards Winter, and in the Druid ceremony a wheel is passed around the circle in symbol of the turning year. The Christian version of this festival is Lammas, which has recently been revived in some churches. The word Lammas comes from hlafmasse – 'loaf-mass' – since bread is offered from the newly harvested grain.

September 21st – Autumnal Equinox

The Autumnal Equinox, on September 21st or thereabouts, is called Alban Elfed or Light of the Water in the Druid tradition. It represents the second of the harvest festivals – this time marking the end of harvest-time, just as Lughnasadh marked its beginning. Again day and night are equally balanced as they were at the time of the Spring Equinox, but soon the nights will grow longer than the days and Winter will be with us. In the ceremony we give thanks for the fruits of the Earth and for the goodness of the Mother Goddess.

And so the circle completes itself as we come again to the time of Samhuinn – the time of death and of rebirth.

What does it mean to celebrate these festivals? Are we simply trying to revive customs that belong to a different era, and are well forgotten? Those who follow Druidry believe strongly that this is not the case. Just as Christmas and New Year are vital to our psychic health because they give us some measure of the passage of our lives, so -if we incorporate a celebration or recognition of these times – do we find that we develop an increasing sense of peace and place in our world and in our lives.

4.0 Herbal Usage

Many of the HERBS utilized by the Druids are still in use today. Most of these herbs were used because they worked. The reasons they still work today may be augmented by studies and formal trials; however the most effective use is still derived from gathering the whole plant and using it fresh.

Brooklime Veronica beccabunga (Water Pimpernel)

A salad herb or "pot herb," Brooklime was used as an astringent to draw water from tissues, decrease swelling, and promote digestion.

Burdock Arctium latta

A powerful blood purifier then and today Burdock root is an edible "pot herb" cooked as a vegetable or raw, grated in salads. Burdock acts as a diuretic, and supports liver function.

Coltsfoot Tussilago farfara

Still one of the best cough remedies, Coltsfoot leaf and bright yellow flowers are antibacterial, soothing, and expectorant. They are antitussive-hence the name- and prevent coughing.

Cowslip Primula veris (Primrose)

Used as a blood cleanser for rheumatic conditions, Cowslip was also used as an expectorant, for bronchitis and whooping cough. The flowers were used in salves for sunburn and dry skin.

Comfrey Symphytum officinale

Mature leaves were used to promote knitting of bone and for wound healing. Compresses of warm wilted Comfrey leaves ease pain and promote healing of sprains, bruises, strains and swelling.

Dandelion Taraxacum officinale

Druids used Dandelion flowers, leaves, and roots as medicine, just as we do. Bright yellow Dandelion flowers make healing oil for massage and a lovely wine. Dandelion's bright green toothed leaves are eaten young in salads or boiled like spinach. They contain large quantities of potassium, Vitamin A –even more than carrots- and B complex vitamins that provide diuresis, removing toxins from the blood through the kidneys and lowering the blood pressure naturally. Dandelion root contains immune stimulating compounds that are present in the root more in the fall than in spring. The root stimulates the flow of bile and is often used as part of a "liver cleanse," both spring and fall.

Elder Sambucus nigra

Druids considered Elder as one of their most sacred trees. Elder stood for the letter 'r' in their alphabet and on the sacred tree calendar was the month of December. We now know that Elder has powerful healing qualities. Elder flowers are used as washes to soften and whiten the skin. Soaked in warm oil, mixed with beeswax, the flowers become nourishing salve. The white umbelliferous flowers can be eaten in muffins or dipped in batter and fried as fritters. Elder flowers also make a lovely, healthy cordial served over ice chips in spring. Medicinally, the flowers are diuretic, and useful for not only colds but also for allergies.

They are both anti-inflammatory and decongestant. Elderberries are high in healthy anthrocyanin (blue) antioxidants, protecting blood vessel walls. Juice, syrup, tincture, and wine made with Elderberries is strongly antiviral. In fact in 1993, Israeli chemists realized that Elderberries were strikingly effective against influenza virus.

Figwort Scrophularia nodosa

Figwort was used for wasting conditions. Both herb and root clear the lymph and liver. Externally, used as a poultice, Figwort clears the skin and subcutaneous tissues. Rich in manganese, the tincture can be used externally or internally to nourish the skin.

GALIUM family was used as strewing herbs then- and to promote removal of toxins from the body as it is used today:

Clivers Galium aparine (Cleavers, Goosegrass)

Cleavers appears in May as does its cousins, was used to clear the skin of eruptions and remains the best remedy for lymphadenitis.

(Sweet) Woodruff Galium odoratum

Woodruff was used in poultices to soothe skin irritations, and brewed into tea to sooth the stomach, clean the liver, and clear stones from the bladder. The classic ingredient in traditional "May Wine" was made by steeping Woodruff in white wine.

Lady's Bedstraw Galium verum (Cheese rennet)

Lady's Bedstraw was used to stuff mattresses and was thought to have lined the Manger of Jesus. Lady's Bedstraw was used to curdle milk and make cheese. Its yellow flowering tops have been used as dye and to color cheese.

Flax Linum usitatissimum

Seeds of Flax (also called Linseed) were used for food. Oil from the seed was cooked with figs and honey for constipation. Flax oil is utilized today to insure maintenance levels of essential fatty acids which increase metabolism, energy, and staying power. Flax seed oil helps also by lifting the spirits and providing a feeling of health and well-being. Consuming Flax seeds and oil also helps skin seem soft and supple. Flax seeds contain high levels of a lignan which is thought to help prevent cancer and which is anti-viral.

Ground Ivy Nepata hederacea

An ancient plant, Ground Ivy trails long square stems and roots that emit compounds that inhibit growth of surrounding plants; thus, it seems to thrive where nothing else will grow. Although Ground Ivy is considered a "weed" today- I prefer to call it an "Herb underfoot." It really is anti-inflammatory, anti-viral, astringent, and a good expectorant. It inhibits the growth of Epstein-Barr virus: the virus that facilitates some skin tumors to grow.

Hawthorne Crataegus spp.

Hawthorne trees can grow for hundreds of years- with their gnarled twisted trunks. The ancients burned the wood as fuel and collected Hawthorne berries for use as a diuretic, and as a treatment for heart problems. Even today, the Hawthorn is held in reverence, is used in hedges, and can be found near sacred wells in England and Wales. Visited often at night, its branches are festooned with tiny bits of lace and cloth to signify its sacred position on the earth.

Today, Hawthorne is used to improve the blood supply to the heart and as an antioxidant specifically directed to blood vessels, keeping the walls clean. It lowers high blood pressure, and helps the heart pump more efficiently.

Madder Rubia tinctorum (Dyer's weed)

Madder was used to acidify the system and to cleanse the blood. Madder helps to "knit" broken bones, alleviate fever, and supports liver function. It is especially useful for urinary tract infections.

Mandrake Mandragora officinalis

Mandrake was used as an anesthetic and soporific. Although not much evidence is apparent, it is probable that the Druids used Mandrake in combination with Henbane, Ivy, Hops, Wild Lettuce, and Poppy to produce sleep and to engender "trances." The smell of the root was said to be sufficient to cause sleep. The leaves are used in poultices for ulcers.

Meadowsweet Spirea ulmaria (Queen-of-the-Meadow, Bridewort, Bride-of-the-Meadow)

Meadowsweet was used to treat fevers and depression. One of the "strewing" Herbs, Meadowsweet was strewn on the ground during "handfastings" and on chamber floors to freshen the room and repel pests. Interestingly, the scent of the leaf is quite different from the flower. The heady scent of the flower represented courtship, while the sharp smell of the foliage represented marriage.

Mint Mentha sativa

Mint -also a strewing Herb- was used as a "protective herb" for the home and eaten to calm digestion.

Mistletoe European Viscum album (Birdlime, Golden Bough, Holy Wood)

Mistletoe was (and still is) used to treat tumors. One of the sacred HERBS, Mistletoe was gathered only by Druids, who are said to have spread their white cloaks on the ground beneath Mistletoe to protect its fall to earth.

Motherwort Leonurus cardiaca

Motherwort has always been a symbol of the feminine. Summer festivals were occasions to dance with Motherwart in the hair. Motherwort is a bitter mint with a strong taste. Its name connotes association with motherhood and the uterus. Its intensely bitter taste has a calming effect on the sympathetic nervous system- calming heart palpitations. It has long been utilized during menopause for nervousness and hormonal changes.

Nettle Urtica dioica (Cow Itch)

Another ancient plant, Nettles is soothing to skin (after the "nettling" has been neutralized by heat or pressure.) Nettle leaf ointments have been utilized to stop bleeding from wounds and nose bleeds. Nettle leaf stops both internal and external bleeding. The long fibers were woven into cloth when flax was not available. People have eaten

Nettles for centuries as a spring tonic. A "pot Herb," Nettles makes wonderfully nourishing soup. Nettle leaves also contain anti-inflammatory acids that help when used in tea as a tonic to treat hay fever, and joint inflammations. The tea also helps curb excessive menstrual bleeding. There is evidence that Nettle root contains a lectin that deters auto-immune diseases such as lupus, rheumatoid arthritis, and multiple sclerosis.

Oak Quercus spp. (Duir)

Perhaps the most important HERB to the Druids, celebrations and ceremonies were always performed in the presence of an Oak. It was then and is presently used as an astringent.

The inner layer of bark and young leaves were used as a gargle and as treatment for mouth sores and sore throats. The tea brings down fevers and stops internal bleeding. Taken both internally and externally, it shrinks varicose veins. Salve made from Oak shrinks hemorrhoids.

Plantain Plantago major

Then as now, Plantain is an "Herb underfoot," growing along pathways and roads. Used as an ointment or poultice Plantain was said to "draw" inflammation from wounds and swelling from bruises. We still apply "spit" poultices of plantain for mosquito or ant bites and bee stings. It will also draw thorns or splinters from under the skin. Stimulating to the immune system, Plantain helps overcome viral infections. Internally, Plantain's antibiotic and antispasmodic qualities lend itself to treatment of bronchitis, calming coughs and relieving bronchospasm. Because Plantain contains mucilage and tannins in addition to anti-inflammatory and antispasmodic action, it is also useful in treatment of irritable bowel syndrome and other irritations of the intestines.

Selago Lycopodium selago

One of the sacred Herbs, Selago was gathered using strict guidelines. As a moss, Selago develops a double- valve spore case which contains the powdery Herb. Spores were used to absorb fluids from injury, and to treat nosebleeds. Spores were also dusted on skin conditions such as diaper rash. Internally, the whole plant was utilized as a cathartic; the spores as a diuretic for edema and powerful cure for diarrhea. Incidentally, the spores are highly flammable, and were used to create pyrotechnical displays during ceremonies.

Self-Heal Prunella vulgaris (All-Heal, Heart-of-the-Earth)

Self-Heal was gathered at night, during the dark of the moon. It was harvested by the head Druid with his sacred sickle and raised above his head in his left hand. Self-Heal, like Vervain was an alter Herb; used to purify the alter and its celebrants. Its healing uses were determined by its antibacterial action: as a gargle and mouthwash. Its astringent action makes it helpful for diarrhea.

Silver Birch Betula alba

This sacred tree comprises the first letter of the Ogham alphabet and the month of November in the Druid calendar. Its peeling bark, paper thin, was most likely utilized as the first writing paper. The bark contains methyl salicylate (oil of Wintergreen); fragrant and anti-inflammatory. This oil was (and is) rubbed on joints for pain relief. Extract of the whole leaf lowers cholesterol and supports the liver. Birch bark is anti-fungal.

Saint John's Wort Hypericum perforatum

St. John's Wort was used since ancient times for pain (specifically deep nerve pain) hemorrhoids and wound healing. It was used internally for ulcers and inflammations of the bowels. Beautiful red oil is made from the yellow blossoms -steeped in oil in the sun to rub on painful areas, especially the spine.

Thyme Thymus vulgaris,T.serpantine

Thyme has been known since ancient time to have antiseptic properties. Anywhere Thyme grows wild will be a place of great energy. Thyme is helpful for sore throats with accompanying ear pain, and for cough. Gargling with Thyme is very helpful for this. Poultices containing Thyme heal skin irritations; facial washes help clear adolescent skin. Internally, Thyme is both anti-inflammatory and anti-spasmodic; calming irritable bowel and relieving gas.

Valerian Valeriana officinalis (Phu)

Sedative in nature, Valerian was used in ancient times to calm the wounded with healing sleep. Nicknamed because of its disgusting smell, Valerian was also called "all heal" in medieval times. It produces restful sleep without hangover, but can become habit-forming.

Vervain Verbenia officinalis (Enchanter's Herb, Herb of Grace)

Pretty Vervain, with its lilac flowers, was infused in wine or worn on the head during Midsummer festivals. Vervain is anti-inflammatory, and anti- spasmodic, to calm the digestion, and was used to purge stones from the urinary tract. It is a mild diaphoretic and lightens mood.

Wild Basil Calmintha clonopodium

Wild Basil was used like Thyme and Calamint is today, as an anti-bacterial. Useful as a liver and spleen cleanser, Wild Basil helps clear jaundice. Externally, a poultice of Wild Basil can clear eyes. Combined with Rosemary and Lavender, it is helpful for migraine headaches.

Water Horehound Lycopus eruopaeus, L. virginicus (Gypsyweed, Bugleweed)

Water Horehound was used in incense and garlands during ceremonies. Presently, Water Horehound, a square-stemmed Mint is utilized as an astringent and a sedative. It has been shown to exhibit a calming effect on an overactive thyroid.

Willow Salix spp.

Sacred to the Druids, Willow was the letter "s" in the alphabet and the month of February (some sources say March) on their calendar. Willows are often found near ancient burial sites. It is a guardian tree, said to protect all it touches. Willow bark has always been used to alleviate pain; however, in the last century salicylic acid was isolated from the bark, and from that aspirin, the great analgesic and anti-inflammatory medicine was born.

Woad Isatis tinctoria

Woad has antifungal properties, and was utilized as a dye-producing a blue color that was painted on skin fungus such as ringworm. It is thought that Woad was used to paint the skin ceremonially in ancient times, somewhat like tattooing is used today.

5.0 Ceremonies and Rituals

Ceremonies

A group of druids of the Order of Bards Ovates and Druids in the early morning glow of the sun, shortly after having welcomed the sunrise at Stonehenge on the morning of the summer solstice.

Every solitary Druid and Druidic grove conducts its rituals and ceremonies in a unique way. Druidic rituals are designed to align their participants with the spirit imbuing nature.[49] According to the anthropologist Thorsten Gieser, Druidic rituals are best seen not as a set of formalised actions but as "a stance, an attitude, a particular mode of experience and perception which gives rise to a feeling of being-in-the-world, of being part of Nature." The practices of modern Druids typically take place outside, in the daylight, in what is described as "the eye of the sun", meaning around midday. In some cases, they instead perform their rites indoors, or during the night. Druidic rituals usually reflect on the time of year and the changing of the seasons.

The most common form of ritual used for seasonal celebrations is a solitary nature ramble to observe and connect with nature, combined with a personal meditation on the meaning of the season at hand. When larger, group rituals are organized among Druids, the rituals tend to be more elaborate and formally structured, with a fixed ceremonial framework unique to the Druid group, and a central ritual activity that varies with the season. Druids residing in the traditionally Celtic regions of Europe are significantly more likely than Druids residing in other parts of the world to perform their ceremonies and rituals in groups.

In the British Isles, Druid group rituals often involve the participants standing in a circle and begin with a "calling of the quarters", in which a participant draws a circle in the air in a deosil direction to hail the north, south, east, and west, marking out the space in which the ceremony will take place. Libations may be poured onto the ground while a chalice of drink is passed around the assembled participants, again in a deosil direction. Food, often in the form of bread or cake, is also passed around the Druids and consumed. This may be followed by a period of meditation among those assembled. A form of earth energy is then visualised, with participants believing that it is sent for a designated healing purpose. This may be designed to help the victims of a particular event, such as a war or an epidemic, or it might be directed to assist individuals known to the group who are ill or requiring emotional support. After the end of the ceremony, the Druids may remain together to take part in a meal, or visit a nearby pub.

There is no specific dress code for ritual within the Druidic movement; some participants wear ordinary clothes, others wear robes.Some groups favour earth-coloured robes, believing that this links them to the natural world and that it aids them in traveling unnoticed when going about at night. Celtic languages are often employed during ceremonies, as are quotations and material from the Carmina Gadelica. Most use some form of Morganwg's Gorsedd Prayer.

Some Druids also involve themselves in spell-casting, although this is usually regarded as a secondary feature among their practices.

<u>Locations for ritual</u>

The two most common locations for Druid rituals are indoors, at home, at a home altar or shrine (92% of Druids), or outdoors in a private garden or wild space (90% of Druids). Only 48% of world Druids regularly participate in rituals held in publicly viewable spaces, and 18% attend rituals at public monuments or popular tourist destinations such as Stonehenge or Avebury, however, Druids in the British Isles are significantly more likely to do so.

Public rituals in the British Isles frequently take place at formations in the natural landscape or at prehistoric sites, among them megalithic constructions from the Neolithic and Bronze Age or earthworks from the Iron Age. Druids often believe that, even if the Iron Age druids did not build these monuments, they did use them for their rites. Performing rituals at said sites allows many Druids to feel that they are getting close to their ancestors. Druids regard them as sacred sites in part as recognition that prehistoric societies would have done the same.[91] Druids in various parts of Ireland and Britain have reported such sites being home to a "Spirit of the Place" residing there. Many Druids also believe that such sites are centres of earth energy and lie along ley lines in the landscape. These are ideas that have been adopted from Earth mysteries writers like John Michell.

<u>Druidic ritual at Stonehenge in Wiltshire, southern England</u>

In the popular imagination, Druids are closely linked with Stonehenge—a Neolithic and Bronze Age site in Wiltshire, southern England. Although Stonehenge predates the Iron Age and there is no evidence that it was ever used by Iron Age druids, many modern Druids believe that their ancient namesakes did indeed use it for their ceremonies. Druids also use many other prehistoric sites as spaces for their rituals, including stone circles like that at Avebury in Wiltshire. Some Druids have erected their own, modern stone circles in which to perform their ceremonies.[95] Druidic practices have also taken place at Early Neolithic chambered long barrows such as Wayland's Smithy in Oxfordshire,[96] and the Coldrum Long Barrow in Kent. In Ireland, Druids perform ceremonies at one of the island's best known prehistoric sites, the Hill of Tara. In 2000, scholar of religion Amy Hale noted that Druidic rituals at such prehistoric sites were "increasingly more common". She regarded the stone circle as "a symbol of an imagined Celtic past" shared by both Druids and Gorseth Bards. As well as performing group rituals at sites, Druids also visit them alone to meditate, prayer, and provide offerings. Aside from seasonal celebrations, rites of passage can also take place at such sites, such as a Druidic baby-naming ceremony which took place at Kent's Chestnuts Long Barrow.

Attitudes to land and environmental conservation are important to the Druidic world-view.[101] In 2003, Druids performed a ritual at the Hill of Tara to heal the location after road construction took place in the adjacent landscape. Others have carried out rituals at Coldrum Long Barrow to oppose fracking in the landscape. Druids have also involved themselves in tree planting projects.

In the 1990s and early 2000s, the use of a ritual based on the sweat lodge became increasingly popular among some Neo-druids in Ireland and the U.K. Some Druids regard these sweat lodges as "initiatory and regenerative opportunities to rededicate oneself to honouring the Earth and the community of life."This practice is regarded differently by different individuals. Some practitioners regard it as a "revival" of genuine pre-Christian druidic practices, others see it a creative and respectful borrowing from one "native spirituality" into another, and a third school of thought regards it as a form of cultural theft. Native Americans who preserve the sweat lodge ceremonies for their communities have protested the appropriation of the ceremony by non-Natives,[106] increasingly so now that people have been injured, and some have died, in fraudulent sweat lodge ceremonies performed by non-Natives.

Druid History, Mysticism, Rituals, Magic, and Prophecy

6.0 Druid Meditations & Exercises

The Druids were very spiritually oriented and one of the best paths to spiritual growth is meditation. In this chapter are a few typically Druid Meditations.

6.1 The Tree Meditation

This is inspired by the deep peace of the trees, that you can practice, either as a spiritual exercise in its own right, or as a prelude to prayer, ritual or other meditation or movement work.

Its purpose is to help you feel centred and grounded, and to help you deepen your experience of being in your body and in relationship to the natural world. It encourages the flow of life-force, cultivates peacefulness, and harmonises Heart and Mind.

Each element of the meditation may be experienced for as long as you wish, and once you have mastered the simple sequence, you can deepen your experience by dwelling for a longer time on each part of the meditation.

Begin by standing or sitting, and becoming aware of the environment around you. If you are not outside in a natural setting, you can imagine yourself in one – such as a forest or woodland grove.

Now move your awareness to your body, and start to move the focus of your attention slowly down from the top of your head, relaxing into your awareness of your body as you do so. Relax your eyes and mouth, release any tension in the shoulders, and gradually move your awareness down through your torso and legs to the soles of your feet. Feel your feet planted firmly on the earth. Imagine roots travelling deep down into the soil, and sense these great strong roots spreading wide and deep beneath you.

Feel the nourishment and energy from the earth travelling up these roots now, until you sense again the soles of your feet. Feel the energy flowing up your body as you move your awareness slowly, with love and acceptance, up your body: up your legs, your thighs, your torso and arms, your chest, your neck, your head.

When you reach the top of your head, just let go of this movement of awareness and rest in an awareness of just Being… still and calm, breathing in and breathing out.

Now you will move your arms slowly in a particular way, as illustrated in the following diagram, and as described in detail in the text that follows:

When you feel ready, raise your arms, not forwards in front of you, but out to either side of you, palms facing down. Let your arms float up effortlessly as if they doing so of their own volition, floating up until they are parallel to the earth. As they reach this position at shoulder-height, turn your palms to face upward, and as you do this, move your arms back a tiny amount – just a centimetre or so – and enjoy the sensation this gives of opening your chest, your heart: welcoming the world. Imagine your arms and hands are like the first great boughs that mark the beginning of the crown of your tree. Sense the branches and leaves of your crown moving in the sunlight and sky above.

Stay in this position as long as you like, and then slowly move your arms up until your fingertips touch above the top of your head, sensing as you do this the top of the crown of your tree. Enjoy the stretch of this movement, and then retrace the movement: slowly lowering your arms down on either side, palms facing up until they reach shoulder-height, at which point they turn downwards, and continue in one flowing movement down, until fingertips meet at the groin, at the mid-line of your body.

As you move your arms down to this position allow your awareness to move towards the earth and a sense of your roots, and then feel the energy of the earth flowing up the trunk of your tree, in other words your legs, until it reaches your hands, at which point your hands begin to travel, fingertips touching, up the mid-line of your body to your chest. Pause at the chest and let your fingertips touch your body. Then bring your fingertips up to the brow to touch there. Then raise the fingertips right up as high as they can go, to repeat the stretch above your head to the top of your crown.

Stay there as long as you wish, and then repeat the sequence twice more: separating your fingertips and sweeping your hands down with palms up, flipping your palms to face downwards at shoulder level until your fingertips meet just in front of your body, then bringing them up again to touch heart and brow before stretching up to the crown.

On the third and final sequence, after stretching up above your head, lower your arms and bring them to rest on either side of you. Then just rest in stillness for a while, open to your awareness, sensing yourself breathing in and breathing out.

When you are ready to finish this phase, give thanks to the trees, and gradually allow any sense of having roots, branches and leaves to dissolve as you become fully aware of your own body.

At this point you can choose to finish the practice, or you can enter deeper into the stillness, either by sitting down or by staying upright, and using whatever technique you prefer for this phase of meditation.

Alternatively, if you are using this practice as a preliminary to a movement meditation such as Yoga, Tai Chi or Qi Gong, you can now move into that phase of work.

6.2   Connecting with Spirits of Place

Finding and establishing a connection to the spirits of place is integral to Druidry, for nature, both the physical world and human nature are an essential part of the practice.

The Druid seeks to find an honorable relationship with the natural world, with the stones and trees, the waterways, the hedgehogs under the bushes in the backyard, the blackbird that sings at dusk, the next door neighbor.

The spirits of place are just that – the energy, the life force, the song of every living thing in a time and place. For most, Druidry is an animistic tradition, seeing this spirit in all things, from the drying, decaying leaf to the mountain rising out of the plain, the lake at dawn to the spider living in the eaves of the house.

Respect and connection to these spirits is what makes for an honorable relationship, which is what the Druid longs and craves for in an ever increasing society that seems intent on separating itself from the natural world.

To find, establish, or even re-establish that connection with the spirits of place, here are a few helpful hints:-

Find a spot outside, near to where you live, where you feel safe. This should be a spot where you can sit undisturbed. It could be in your backyard, in a local park, in a nearby wood, by a river, or even in a quiet room of your house.

Go to that spot daily, as many times as you can, and listen. Hear the songs around you – the yipping of small children, the pigeons on the chimney, the ambulance sirens, the wind through the trees. Really pay attention to these sounds, hearing everything in your world around you. This is sometimes easier to do with eyes closed, to really focus the concentration.

Don't judge or think about what you hear – just listen. As soon as thoughts start to interfere, you aren't paying attention to other sounds. Really try to hear the spirits of place.

Next, feel the space around you. Are you sitting on the ground, on a bench, standing on a large stone? Reach out with your fingertips and feel those things around you. You can also feel with your feet the surface you stand on, or your backside the ground you sit upon. Feel the wind on your face, the sunshine on your shoulders, the rain falling upon your head. Again, try not to let thoughts distract you from feeling.

Continuing with the senses, now open up your awareness of scent, and really smell the air that surrounds you, the grass beneath your feet, the honeysuckle, the woodsmoke. Continue working with scent much like the previous senses.

Finally, look around you at everything that surrounds you. Pay attention to the minute detail in a changing leaf, the bee exploring the hibiscus, the cat lounging in the sunshine. You'll be surprised at what you have missed previously if you really pay attention. Your backyard could become a whole new world!

Now that the senses have been opened to your surroundings, it is time to open your heart, your soul, your song to the spirits of place. After paying attention to the other spirits of place, find that spot within yourself which craves for relationship with the natural world. Open it up and let it sing along with the other spirits that you have explored. Don't drown out the other sounds – the key thing to remember is to work with respect. Let your soul open like a flower towards the morning sun, and in an open and friendly manner, become part of your surroundings.

Remembering that you are a part of your natural world, and not separate from it, is critical. Doing these exercises at least once a day can really help to establish that connection that we crave with our natural world. Whatever the weather, whatever the season, keep going back to that place, preferably outside.

Within the home, establishing a connection with the spirits of place is just as important, however. The same exercises can be performed indoors, listening to the central heating or the crackle of the hearthfire, feeling the carpet or the rug beneath our feet, smelling the laundry drying on the rack and looking at the shadows playing upon the wall.

Getting to know your house, and its spirit, is a very important part of connecting with the spirits of place, for your house is your sanctuary – it keeps you safe and warm and protected from the elements. Here are a few other ideas for finding a connection with the spirits of place within the home:-

Build an altar in your home. Place upon it things that reflect for you the connection that you wish to establish, or things that you find beautiful and inspiring. It could be as simple as a bowl of earth with bits from the garden that you have gathered, with a candle set in the middle. It could be pictures of loved ones, ancestors, or even pets. Feathers, stones gathered from long walks, anything that makes you want to come back to it is suitable. Spend time at your altar, doing the above exercises, finding the spirits of place in the home.

Leave offerings to the spirits of place, whether inside or outside the home. A bit from every meal, a piece of music that you have written and played, a beverage or even burning a special incense can all be offerings to help and establish that relationship.

Giving and receiving are an essential part of any relationship, and you can show your appreciation and your gratitude for what you have through the process of leaving offerings.

The spirits of place consist of the community as well, so try to help out with your community. Aiding at a local shelter, picking up litter, building bat boxes, donating to charities – all of these can help further that relationship with your world around you.

May you be blessed in your new relationship!

6.3 The Garden Meditation

The concept here is to explore one's own inner landscape.

It is time set aside to explore our imagination. Instead of looking for patterns using runes or tarot, or looking for omens in the outer-world, we can at any time look inward, finding patterns and symbols, messages and even omens in our own subconscious mind, within our own imagination. In this meditation we create a garden. It can be any garden and we can change it at will.

It is understood this garden is a reflection of our own being. It is 100% ours. Images in this garden represent aspects of ourselves. This meditation comes from the Hawaiian Huna tradition but variations of it are found all around the globe. I learned a very similar concept from Bobcat which she refers to as "the inner grove".

The garden can be used for a tool for healing as well, setting patterns in our subconscious mind that will manifest in our physical being. An example is this: we may be ill with a chest cold; in our garden a stream runs through the garden; when we do the meditation, the stream is blocked with weeds, silt, branches, and other materials. During the meditation we clean out the blockages. We re-envision the garden stream as free flowing, clear and beautiful. Our mind sees this as the natural order of things and begins to manifest this in our body. We get healthy.

To me, this inner garden doesn't just represent my physical body. I meet guides there. I do shamanic work.

Within your garden you may have helpers too, gnomes, elves, fairies, a human gardener – again, it doesn't matter. You can tell them what you want to change and they will do the work. You are all powerful here as it is yours, totally and completely. The important thing is to make it feel real.

Use your senses while you are there. Start with touching three things, tasting three things, smelling three things, but try eventually to use all your senses. If you don't like the garden change it to something completely different. But at first just see what your mind throws out at you. Try not to be overly willful. Let your mind show you things.

I highly recommend journaling about your garden. It is interesting and can be very insightful to see how the garden changes and evolves over time.

You can use this meditation for the following:

Relaxation; Interpretation – as a way to check in with your inner landscape (subconscious mind, your body, your soul) ; and Resolution – everything in your garden is a reflection of what is going on in your life. Your garden can help you understand this better; you may see relationships that aren't apparent in your daily work. Here is a place where you can correct issues and plant seed of change.
The meditation is done as follows:

1. As with all time we use for our spiritual practices, it is important to begin by making prayers to the spirits of place, giving thanks for the space you have and asking that your meditation be undisturbed. Begin the process of bringing yourself fully into the moment and into the place where you are. Find yourself comfortable and relaxed, rooting into the Earth. Become aware of your breath. Don't force it. Let it flow in and out without effort. Be aware of the process and feel the movement of the air into your body and back out into the world. Use your breath to feel your roots growing deeply into the Earth, seeking strength and nourishment.

Think about who you are in this place at this moment. Feel the edges of your nemeton, your intimate space. Become fully present. Close your eyes. Let your breath flow naturally, leading you into meditation.

(If you are having a difficult time relaxing, proceed anyway as the process of doing the Garden meditation will naturally relax you. Close your eyes and take a deep breath. Blow the air out and let it naturally come back into your body. Then just breath naturally, unforced.)

2. Let an image of a garden come into your mind. Don't worry if it isn't clear and well developed. Don't judge what comes into your mind. If you feel that it is easier to travel to your garden somehow (riding magical creatures, flying, using a boat, whatever), feel free to use that imagery but let the image arise naturally. In your mind find yourself inside of that garden. The garden can be anything, a farm, flower garden, forest, jungle, a Victorian paradise, whatever. It doesn't matter. Fill it with anything you want, a sacred well, stone walls, statues, water fountains, and water gardens, endless flowers, wind chimes, well maintained lawns, a Zen garden of stone and sand, anything. It can just be totally natural as well (mine is a jungle). Don't judge what comes into your imagination. It is just your mind's creation. It is a place to start and nothing is fixed. The garden represents your subconscious and your physical body. It is a place where you can make change.

3. Once in your garden bring your senses into play. Touch three things, smell three things, and hear three things (bird song, waterfalls, rivers and streams, the wind through the trees, the texture of a stone, explore it with your senses). If there is a stream, well, or fruit, smell and taste the water or fruit. Explore the texture of things. What sounds are on the

wind? Bring as much of your consciousness into play as you can.

4. Move and explore your garden. What grows there? What is the soil like? What is the climate? What is the time of year? Let your curiosity lead you around. What are you wearing? How do you feel in this place?

5. If there is change you wish to make in your garden, do the work now. If the work is more than can be done in a moment, express the intention of the change you seek. If you have helpers in the garden, let them know the work that needs to be done. Begin the process of that change.

6. Within your garden, find a focal point such as a tree or fountain, or stone. This is an inner landmark that will help you get back to your garden quickly when you need to meditate and don't have a lot of time. Become familiar with it. Work with it until it becomes "real".

7. When you are ready to leave, bless you garden, bless your helpers. Bring your emotional presence into play. Feel the gratitude within your own soul and express the thanks outwardly. This is your place of beauty and possibility.

8. When you are ready to end the meditation, do so consciously, not from distraction. Find yourself present again on the physical plane. Become aware again of the spirits of place. Give thanks that you have had a place of solitude to do this work. Give thanks that you were not disturbed. Find your roots again, feeling the Earth beneath you given you constant support. When you are ready, move on with your day.

7.0 The Tree Alphabet

'Darach' means Oak in Gaelic so 'Darach Croft' means 'Oak Croft' (although technically it should be croit na daraich). However, there are other Gaelic words to describe an Oak, such as 'Dair' or 'Duir' which come from the more ancient Ogham (OH-am) alphabet. Ogham was predominantly used to write the early Irish language and from the 6th century was used in the Gaelic kingdom of Dalriada covering what is now Argyll, West Lochaber and the Inner Hebrides as well as the northern tip of Ireland. The Tree Alphabet was also used by the Druids in its more ancient form called the Ogham Alphabet.

The Gaelic Tree Alphabet

A is for Ailm (pronounced 'A-lum') and is predominantly associated with Elm, but also Pine and Fir

These tall straight trees are associated with perspective and height. In ancient Celtic tree lore, the Elm is intimately bound up with death and the transition into the Underworld, whilst evergreen Fir trees were associated with the healing of a person's inner soul. The kind of elm that grows most widely in Scotland is Wych Elm. This refers not to witches, who were said to shun Elm trees, but refers to its flexibility taken from an Old English verb meaning 'to give way'. As wood from the Elm is very flexible it consequently does not make a good material to construct buildings from. However, like Alder it does withstand water very well, so it has been popular in making boat hulls, bridges and wheels. Like Scots Pine, hollowed out elm has previously been used as water piping before the advent of metal water pipes. Elm is also the material that coffins were traditionally made from. Welsh longbows too, were often made from Elm, whereas English longbows were more commonly made from Yew.

B is for Beith (pronounced 'BAE-yh') and is associated with Birch (particularly Silver Birch)

Known as 'The Lady of the Woods', in Celtic Mythology Birch represents purification, change and new beginnings, femininity, grace, purity, family connections, protection, healing, new life and rebirth. As Birch is one of the first trees to come into leaf it would be an obvious choice as a representation of the emergence of spring. The Birch is known as a 'Pioneer Tree' meaning that it can restart the colonisation of woodlands after long term natural disasters. According to Scottish Highland folklore, a barren cow herded with a birch stick would become fertile.

Birch bark was used for tanning leather whilst Birch wood is tough, heavy and straight-grained, and was historically used to make infants cradles, cabinets and furniture. It is also used to make besom brooms, the archetypal witches' broomsticks upon which they were said to fly (maybe due to the consumption of Fly Agaric mushrooms that typically grow beneath Birch trees in Autumn).

C is for Coll (pronounced 'Col') and is associated with Hazel

In Celtic mythology Hazel is associated with wisdom, creativity and knowledge. The Hazel is one of the very oldest native British trees. Traces of hazelnut shells and pollen have been discovered in cave settlements, dating back around 10,000 years.

Pliable, straight shoots called 'withies' grow up from the base and these are still cut for walking sticks and pinned into shape whilst growing, for shepherd's crooks. Pilgrims often used to make staffs from Hazel, providing a sturdy walking stick and a means of self-defense. Hazel was also often used in weaving of baskets in medieval times.

August is known as the Hazel Moon as this is when Hazel nuts appear on the trees. The red spots on wild salmon were said to have been gained from the fish having consumed nine hazelnuts that fell into a pool from a surrounding grove.

D is for Dair (or Duir) (pronounced 'Dahr') and is associated with Oak

In Celtic mythology and lore, the Oak is associated with strength, resilience and self-confidence and is a great tree for enhancing inner strength, especially when you have experienced a great loss in life. It is said that the oak tree helps builds strength, resilience and self-confidence, and lends power so you might rebuild your life and move forward.

Oak has been valued for its strength and durability, and was commonly used in construction of homes and the bark has been used in the tanning industry. St. Columba was said to have had a fondness and respect for Oak trees and to have been reluctant to fell them, although his early chapel on Iona was constructed of Oak from the nearby Mull Oakwoods.

A well-known Celtic symbol is the Dara Celtic Knot, usually featuring an interwoven design that represents the root system of an ancient Oak. Like other Celtic knots, the Dara Knot is made up of intertwined lines with no beginning or end.

E is for Eadha (pronounced 'EH-ga') and is associated with Aspen

Aspen is seen as a symbol of endurance, courage and the overcoming of obstacles. In the Highlands of Scotland, the Aspen was often rumored to be connected to the realm of the Faeries and the Gaelic name Strontian, where the croft is located, is Sròn an t-Sithein meaning 'Nose (or point) of the Faerie Hill. There was a Highland tradition of not using the wood from the Aspen for fishing or agricultural implements, or in house construction, suggesting that the Aspen was considered a faerie tree on a par with the Rowan Tree, the use of whose wood holds similar taboos. However, Aspen wood is very lightweight and when dried, becomes very buoyant, and was therefore historically a popular choice for oars and paddles. Weight for weight it also offers unrivalled protection and was the wood of choice for shields and armour. In Celtic mythology Aspen was also seen as providing spiritual protection as well, and the unique shape of the leaves creates a whispering sound in a breeze, which the Celts believed was the souls of their ancestors communicating.

F is for Feàrn (pronounced 'Fyaarn') and is associated with Alder

In Celtic Mythology Alder is often associated with water, secrecy, nature, bad luck, spirituality, and balance. Alder trees were also a source of great mystery to the Celts as their sap turns a deep red when exposed to the air, as if they could bleed when cut.

In Irish mythology Deirdre of the Sorrows fled to Alba (Scotland) with Naoise, son of Usna, to escape the wrath of the King of Ireland, Conchobhar mac Nessa to whom Deirdre had been betrothed. They are said to have hidden in the Alder woods of Glen Etive, contributing in part to the themes of hiding and secrecy connected with Alder in Celtic lore.

The wood from the Alder is oily and water resistant, turning hard when under water and so survives being submerged very well. Consequently and was often used for construction of buckets, water pipes, the foundations for bridges and other construction in wet conditions. Parts of Venice in Italy are built on top of Alder piles which were driven in to the Venetian lagoon. In Scotland crannochs (wooden strongholds built over the water of Scottish lochs) were built on rafts or piles of Alder trunks.

Like the Birch tree, Alder is considered to be a 'pioneer' tree, as it is often the first to colonize wet and treeless ground or to heal landscapes disturbed by fire, flood, clear cuts, or storms. It also has a unique characteristic that greatly improves the soil around it over the course of its life. The Alder forms a symbiotic relationship with a particular type of soil bacteria that takes up residence in their roots which have nitrogen fixing nodules in them. This bacteria enables the Alder to make better use of the nitrogen in the air, in return for which the Alder provides the soil bacteria with sugar. Its deep root system also helps to increase stability in river banks and other damp areas where the tree thrives.

A green dye can be derived from the flowers and was used to colour and thus camouflage the garments of outlaws such as Robin Hood, as well as the clothes of faeries, concealing them from human eyes.

G is for Gort (pronounced 'GOR-ht') and is associated with Ivy

In Celtic Mythology Ivy is often associated with prosperity and growth, and it is believed to be a bringer of good fortune, particularly to women. Allowing it to grow up the outside walls of your home was thought to protect inhabitants from magic and curses. However, if it should die or fall down then misfortune would befall those who lived there. Ivy represented peace to the Druids who often related the Ivy with peace because of its ability to bind different plants together. It was frequently carried by young women for good luck and fertility, and today Ivy is often used at weddings, where it is seen to symbolize fidelity. The Faeries are reputed to love Ivy as, along with Heather, is said not to grow in the Faerie Realm accounting for why they like it so much.

H is for Huath (pronounced 'HOO-er') and is associated with Hawthorn

In Celtic Mythology the thorns of the Hawthorn are often associated with cleansing, protection and defense, although the stem of the Hawthorn is seen to bring bad luck if brought into the home. This is thought to be due to the fact that many species of Hawthorn give off a smell of death and decay when cut. Often called the Faerie Tree for it is said to guard the entrance to the faerie realm, the Scottish mystic and poet, Thomas the Rhymer, was said to have met the Faerie Queen under a Hawthorn tree. Having accompanied her into the faerie realm, he returned to find that he had been absent for seven years. In Celtic mythology the Hawthorn was one of the most likely trees to be inhabited by faeries, and it was said that Hawthorn trees could not be cut down or damaged in any way without incurring the often fatal wrath of their supernatural guardians. In Celtic Mythology, Faeries were not friendly little creatures that lived at the bottom of your garden but were feared and respected, with tales of kidnapping and curses abound, so the Hawthorn was usually treated with care and respect.

The famous Holy Thorn Hawthorn that grows on Glastonbury Tor is said to be a descendant of the one that grew where Joseph of Arimethea thrust his staff into the ground.

I is for Iogh (pronounced 'Yoo') and is associated with Yew

The Yew tree has come to symbolize death and resurrection in Celtic culture, perhaps because drooping branches of old Yew trees can root and form new trunks where they touch the ground or because of its unusual growth pattern, in which new growth forms inside the old. Alternatively it might be because the Yew has no medicinal value at all, and almost all parts of it are toxic to humans and animals. However, Yew trees themselves are capable of living thousands of years and aged ones are often found in churchyards or in places that had pre-Christian spiritual significance. The Fortingall Yew in Perthshire is thought to be between 2,000 and 3,000 years old (some say more) and is thought be one of the oldest trees in Britain if not in Europe..

The Yew produces a very hard, close-grained wood that has commonly been used in furniture making, but is perhaps best known as the material from which English longbows were made. The Scots also used yew longbows sometimes and Robert the Bruce is said to have ordered bows to be made from the sacred yews at Ardchattan Priory in Argyll that were then used during the Scots' victorious battle at Bannockburn in 1314.

L is for Luis (pronounced 'LOO-sh') associated with Rowan

The Rowan Tree (also known as the Mountain Ash) is often associated with humanity, perseverance, and life as well as insight, blessings and protection against enchantments and magic. Celtic druids believed that women were forged from the Rowan tree (as men were forged from the Ash tree) and so the Rowan symbolizes the fragility of life, motherhood, birth, blood, protection, and survival.

Rowan trees are not tall and hence do not often grow in amongst taller trees, so are more commonly found growing singly. However, they can grow in shallow soil and at high altitude, making them common in the Scottish Highlands, often at altitudes where few other trees will grow. As the Celts believed that the veil between the heavens and the mortal world was thinnest on top of mountains where the land was closest to Heaven, this is perhaps why the Rowan has a special spiritual significance in Celtic Mythology.

The wood from the Rowan is strong and resilient, making excellent walking sticks, and was also often used for tool handles, spindles and spinning wheels. However, it is widely reputed to be unlucky to cut down a Rowan. A black dye can be extracted from the young tree bark, which contains a lot of tannin.

M is for Muin (pronounced 'MOO-n') and is commonly associated with the Vine, but also with the Bramble

Muin is a symbol of inward journeys and life lessons learned. There is disagreement about whether Muin should be associated with the Vine, which although featured in Bronze Age art, isn't native, arriving in Britain when the Romans introduced wine 2000 years ago. The Bramble on the other hand is native to the cooler climate of Northern Europe and shares the winding characteristics and bares fruit like the vine. In Gaelic the Bramble is known as Dris-Muine, which means 'Prickle Thorn', further supporting this theory. This is why the Ogham Muin can represent either the Vine or the Bramble.

The Vine is a symbol of both happiness and wrath and is connected to prophecy and truthful speaking, perhaps because of the behaviors of those under the influence of fermented grapes used to make wine. The Bramble is most commonly associated with Devil and it was said that the Celts didn't eat Blackberries as the Devil had spat on them. The association with Satan is also present in Christian mythology, where it was said that when Satan was banished from the Kingdom of Heaven, he fell in to a patch of brambles and cursed them as they pierced him. Goats are one of the few animals that eat brambles, and they are traditionally associated with Satan in Christianity, perhaps adding to the negative associations of the Devil with Brambles.

N is for Nuin (pronounced 'NOO-n') and is associated with the Ash tree

The Ash tree has long been a symbol with wisdom, knowledge, and divination. Celtic druids also believed that men were forged from the Ash tree (and women from the Rowan) contributing to its association with masculinity, strength and rebirth. In a number of legends, the Ash is connected to the gods, and considered sacred. In Norse legend, Yggdrasil, the World Tree, is considered to be an Ash tree with its root reaching far down into the Underworld, and its trunk reaching up into the heavens, and its branches spreading out across all the countries on Earth. The Norse God Odin hung from Yggdrasil for nine days and was rewarded with insight and wisdom.

Ash has historically been seen to have healing and protective properties. In British folklore newborn babies were often given a spoonful of Ash sap whilst placing Ash berries in a cradle was thought to protect the child from being taken away as a changeling by mischievous Faeries.

Most recently, Ash wood was used to make stagecoach axles as it was said to bear more weight than any other wood. Further back in history spear shafts were often made of Ash, as were bows where Yew wood was not available. The Old Norse for an Ash tree was 'Askr' and for a spear was 'Atgeir' so who knows, Asher may have meant spear maker!

O is for Onn (pronounced 'OH-n') and is associated with Gorse

In Celtic Mythology, Gorse (also known as Furze) was thought to provide protection against misfortune (and spiteful faeries - see below) and was also associated with resilience, optimism, as well as with the Sun, light, and fire. It seeks sunshine and warmth and is quick to sprout new shoots. To this day, it is often cleared using a controlled burn to allow new gorse to come through. In folklore there was a belief that protection from spiteful faeries could be achieved by completely barricading the space around your bed with gorse branches!

Gorse wood burns at a high temperature with a fierce flame, similar to charcoal, and for this reason it was often used as a fuel. The flowers of the gorse are bright yellow and can be used as a yellow dye for clothes. The gorse generally flowers from January to June, although it can flower sporadically throughout the year.

P is for Peith Bhog (pronounced 'Payh fvog') and is associated with Downy Birch

As previously mentioned when describing Beith, in Celtic Mythology birch was traditionally associated with birth, love and purity. Birch was often placed over cradles to keep the young safe from evil spirits and bundles of birch twigs were used to drive out the spirits of the old year.

Downy Birch is more upright than silver birch and the bark is browner in colour with more obvious horizontal grooves and lacking the papery quality of the Silver Birch. Silver

Birch has hairless and warty shoots whereas downy birch shoots are covered in small, downy hairs. The range of Downy Birch is more northerly and westerly than silver birch, and it can grow at higher elevations. It can grow further north than any other broadleaf species. In the spring, the sap from the Downy Birch can be used to make refreshing drinks, wines, and ales.

R is for Ruis (pronounced 'Roosh') and is associated with Elder

Elder is often seen as representing endings, transitions and maturity in terms of the awareness that comes with experience. In both Celtic and wider British folklore, Elder is said to provide protection against malevolent faeries, witches and the Devil. It was thought that if you burned the wood from the Elder, you would see the Devil, but if you planted Elder by your house it would keep the Devil away. Traditionally, it was said that the best protection for a home was obtained by having a Rowan tree by the front door and an Elder tree at the back door.

Elder wood is hard and off-white. The mature wood is good for whittling and carving, while smaller stems can be hollowed out to make craft items such as beads or musical instruments. It is reputed that the Faery Folk love music and merrymaking, and most of all they like the music from instruments made of elder wood. Elder foliage was once used to keep flies away and branches were often hung around dairies in the belief that it would stop the milk from 'turning'. The flowers can be used to make wine, cordial or tea.

Whilst the Elder is not a common tree in Scotland, many parts of the tree were used for dying in the Harris tweed industry, with blue and purple dyes being obtained from the berries, yellow and green dyes from the leaves, and grey and black dyes from the bark.

S is for Suil (pronounced 'Sool') and is associated with Willow

In Celtic culture and lore, the Willow was associated with knowledge, optimism, adaptability and spiritual growth. The ease with which a new tree can be grown merely by pushing a healthy branch cutting into the soil has come to symbolize renewal, growth, vitality and immortality in other parts of the world.

Willow trees were an important part of Celtic Mythology, and were thought of as sacred because they grow mostly on riverbanks and on the sides of lochs, both of which held special spiritual significance. Borders were important in Celtic culture, with the Rowan the most sacred for bordering the earth and the heavens, with Willow significantly going on the border between land and water.

Whilst in many cultures, the Willow has been associated with sadness and mourning, this was not the case in Celtic culture where Willow was known for its ability to relocate after being uprooted, either by nature or by man.

Much like the Alder, Willows are pioneer trees and they spread roots helping to stop soil erosion along banks in their natural, watery habitats. Willow has been harvested for wicker work and baskets, small coracles, and even bee hives were constructed with this bendable, flexible wood.

Most famously they are used in the construction oil cricket bats and stumps. In the Nineteenth century, scientists discovered that the Willow contains salicylic acid, which is similar to the active ingredient in Aspirin.

T is for Teine pronounced 'TEEN-uh') and is associated with Holly

As an evergreen, Holly was connected with immortality and a symbol of fertility and regeneration. Felling an entire Holly tree was said to have brought bad luck. However, the use of sprigs for decoration has always been allowed and holly has variously been brought into the house to protect the home from malevolent faeries or to allow faeries to shelter in the home without friction between them and the human occupants. Holly trees were also said to protect dwellings from lightning strikes if planted close to the home.

In folklore the Holly was King of the Woods for half the year, ruling from the summer to the winter solstices, at which time Holly was defeated by the Oak King who ruled until the Summer Solstice again. In this way Holly was seen as the rival of Oak for the favor of the Lady of the Woods, Birch, who switched her allegiance from Oak to Holly and then back again.

Whilst it now rare to see fully grown Holly trees, and more common to find it in hedges or as part of Oak or Beech woodland, large pieces of Holly wood have been used in furniture making and smaller pieces being used to make walking sticks. Holly wood is very heavy and hard, though fine grained, and is one of the whitest of all types of wood.

U is for Ur (pronounced 'OohS') and is associated with Heather

Heather symbolizes luck, healing, passion and generosity, with flowers that are full of nectar and so attractive to bees, which are themselves seen as messengers between the spirit world and the mortal realm. In Scotland it competes with the thistle to be the most iconic plant where it is often seen as the Highland equivalent of the four-leafed clover, especially white heather. However, it is sometimes considered unlucky if brought indoors, though it could be used in this manner as a protection against witches. It has been said that the Faerie Folk live in the heather bells and honey from heather is their favorite food. Heather, like Ivy is said not to grow in the Faerie Realm accounting for why they like it so much.

The Celts often referred to heather as a plant of attraction, romance and intoxication. Ale and mead were made using heather, explaining the intoxication, but it also had many other practical uses. Heather was used in thatching homes, broom-making, rope-twisting, basket-weaving and making dyes. The Picts were said to have made a fine ale from heather alone, without the addition of malt, hops (which don't grow in Scotland) or any other sweetener, relying exclusively on the heather blooms and their nectar for the flavor, and to fuel the fermentation process.

8.0 Druidic Magic

Celtic legends are full of accounts of magic and spell-casting ~ magical mists that blind enemies, rains of fire, curses that maim and injure, healing wells, cauldrons that resurrect the dead, people who transform themselves or others into animals etc.

In this chapter we will aim to look at some of the attitudes towards, and philosophies behind the very concept of, magic. First of all, what do we mean by magic? There is no clear-cut answer to this, but generally it can be taken as the ability to cause change in the world by means that currently defy scientific explanation. The means by which the change is instigated usually has no obvious causal link to the change ~ there is no reason yet offered by science as to why chanting particular words should cure a disease, or why wearing an engraved piece of wood should enable the wearer to pass unnoticed.

There are innumerable books which convey the impression that wealth, romance and vibrant health can be had in exchange for prancing about a purple candle at the full moon. Clearly if it were that easy the world would be a far happier place than it currently is. Magic is not easy, and it cannot be learnt in five simple steps for a mere £4.99! Whilst magic can be used to heal or to aid with personal problems, it is perhaps best conceived of as a method of spiritual transformation.

Different cultures have varying stances on the nature and purpose of magic, none of which are mutually exclusive. The Ancient Egyptians held to the doctrine of Heka, the notion that the universe is created by the power of the spoken word. In this belief all things have their Ren, or True Name (distinct from the mundane name used in daily life.) To correctly pronounce the True Name of a person or thing was to create, or perhaps more appropriately recreate, it; to influence, shape and transform. It may well be that the original Druids also held to a similar idea, but if they did it has not survived the passage of time in written form.

What does come across as a dominant theme in Celtic mythology is the importance attached to shape-shifting, often called fath-fith. Whilst the Egyptian magician spoke the universe, the Celt became it. In becoming a hawk, deer etc, the magician experiences life from a profoundly different viewpoint. Faced with a challenge the Druid becomes the thing most suited to deal with it. Whilst the stories treat the changes as physical ones, the modern reader is more likely to comprehend them as psychological change ~ entering a trance state and taking on the identity and mental patterns of another living creature. Clearly such a thing requires a massive amount of mental discipline and practice, and cannot be learnt from some codswallop book or by forking out a small fortune to go on some dire course.

Falling in love, seeing a spectacular waterfall etc are often described as magical experiences ~ meaning there is something wonderful, awe-inspiring and numinous about them. The accomplished worker of ritual magic will know that a ritual also needs to have that aura of profound excitement (or trembling dread, depending on the nature of the magic) about it for it to work. A bland, prosaic ritual will produce no effect worthy of mention. One can but wonder how many people these days find their lives to be magical, wondrous, and mysterious. In 2006 over 31 million prescriptions were written for various anti-depressants and mood enhancing drugs, costing the NHS approximately 411.1 million pounds. Clearly a large number of people find life desperately bland and unhappy. Ritual magic is far more to do with awakening to the glory of life than it is to do with the Hollywood nonsense of lightning bolts flashing out of wands.

Virtually all ancient cultures have accepted the idea that magic is real. There are varied accounts for how it happens, but many feature the idea of some sort of mysterious power or energy that mystics and magicians can tap into. Some cultures see this force as benevolent and positive, others as neutral and morally akin to electricity ~ in that electricity will still work regardless of whether it is being used to power a life-support machine or to torture someone to death. Unfortunately so much of early Celtic philosophy has been lost that we no longer have a complete or reliable picture as to exactly how the early Druids conceived of magical power.

Modern books on magic tend to emphasize ideas heavily influenced by the development of psychology since the work of Freud. Here magic is seen as primarily a matter of self-belief, where the intention of the magician is far more important than the ritual trappings of colored candles, incense, talismans etc. If the magician believes it will work, then it will ~ regardless of what tools may be used. In this approach, all the candles, robes, herbs etc are basically theatrical window dressing to support what goes on in the magician's head.

Certainly practical experience shows that placebo is a strong factor in magic, particularly where a problem can largely be solved by putting someone at their ease or trying to achieve a change in mental state ~ spells to make people more confident etc.

A person who believes herself to be ugly and unattractive will behave in ways that discourage contact from others, which will then reinforce the notion that no-one fancies her in the first place. If her self-image changes, then her behavior is likely to change ~ she will act in a confident, outgoing manner that is likely to attract attention. She may start dressing differently, being more talkative, attending new places etc. Plus she is likely to notice when people are flirting with her, rather than wallowing in self-pity and dismissing friendliness as mere patronizing kindness. For such a person, casting a "love spell" may be more a case of transforming her self-image than necessarily of conjuring cosmic forces.

Several ancient cultures believed that some things had their own innate power, independent of the magician. So there is a Germanic story of a man who accidentally caused a woman to fall ill by carving the wrong runes on a talisman ~ regardless of what he intended the talisman to do, the runes worked their own magic.

There is evidence that the insular tribes favored this approach, regarding certain things (such as trees, rocks, ogam letters etc) as having a power all their own, which the magician could not change or over-ride. The Druid exists in a world full of spirits ~ even if he does not call directly on a god to work a spell, he will be in a particular place whose bocanach may or may not support the spell; may wave a wand that has a sentient spirit; may stand near a bonfire that is alive and watching what goes on etc. All these spirits may choose to help, hinder, or ignore the spell being woven. It would be a foolish Druid who decided to work magic without bothering to first check if the spirits around him were in harmony with his aims.

Can a spell to cure a cancerous tumor be cured by placebo alone? If it could then, arguably, that power would be pretty damned magical in itself. However, most people would suggest that the ability to dispel a tumor requires more than just a bit of nebulous "positive thinking". It suggests the presence of a very real magical force that can make a measurable change in the body. Various cultures around the world have given this force a name ~ the Far Eastern countries speak of chi or ki, for example. It is uncertain what name the old Druids would have used for this power, assuming they even had such a concept in the first place. A popular term (since the publishing of Iolo Morgannwg's colorful book Barddas in 1862, which gave the word a new spin) is nwyfre ~ the Welsh word for sky.

This is related to the word for holiness and sacred essence. Some have argued that this is due to Christian influence, and the whole child-like idea of Jehovah being up in the clouds (though equally it can be argued that the Christians acquired that idea from Greek religion, given that the storybook idea of Jehovah as an old beardie in a white robe sitting on a cloud derives from Zeus.) However, other linguists have pointed out that the old word nemeton (sacred place) contains the association with sky, suggesting a place open to the air. In one of the versions of the Lebor Gabala, the Tuatha descended from the sky and landed on the Iron Mountain in County Leitrim. Though medieval Christianity heavily influences the Lebor, it forms part of a pattern that suggests an old link between the sky and concepts of sanctity.

There is no suggestion from the old texts that other Welsh writers used the word nwyfre to mean "magic power", but that is the context that it is increasingly used in these days. In Gaelic the comparable word is neamh.

Some writers prefer to use the word anam, which simply means spirit or soul. Yet others (especially those in OBOD) use the Welsh term awen, or its Gaelic equivalent of ai or imbas. All these words mean poetic inspiration, the sudden flash of the Muse that grants an artistic vision. In the medieval story of Taliesin, awen is actually a potion brewed up by Ceridwen. In the Irish tale of Fionn (with which there are decided resemblances) a similar power comes to the young hero when he accidentally imbibes the juices of the Salmon of Wisdom. Both have the idea of this transcendent force being a liquid, and in both stories it is accidentally consumed rather than going to the person for whom it was intended. This could suggest the use of some sort of concoction, perhaps a hallucinogenic. It might suggest an influence of the Christian notion of Divine Grace, which is visited upon people whether they appear to deserve it or not ~ or it may reflect an older idea that magical talent is transferred in some very curious way, unrelated to the amount of work an individual has put into study etc (a concept that may well appeal to the bone idle student.)

Whatever term you wish to use is largely down to personal preference, given that we have (as yet) no concrete ideas as to what terms the early Druids themselves used. The underlying ideas tend to be rather similar ~ the concept that there is a power that moves through the universe, which can be harnessed by some people who know the arcane techniques and grants them amazing insights and understandings.

The Egyptians regarded Heka as an innate presence within the universe and believed a deity of the same name regulated it. It's quite possible that one of the Old Gods of the British tribes may once have been regarded as the origin or regulator of this dynamic power that turns gormless farm-boys into Chief Bards.

How a magical force, of whatever name, might work is difficult to say, given that we are only recently beginning to look at magic seriously again. Some of it may be argued as instigating changes in the mind, such as the previously mentioned love spell. Some may be direct changes at a physical level ~ such as the other case of banishing a tumor.

Like most old stories, the Celtic tales reflect magic being used to help or harm. In the latter case, magic is seen to affect people against their will. This clearly raises a raft of ethical issues for modern Druids that have been of less concern in the distant past. The stories suggest that people were largely unconcerned about violating freewill; if it was done to advance one's own tribe against enemy tribes. These days' people tend to be far less comfortable with such things, and generally speaking few of us are likely to be drawn into "battle magic" situations. Largely due to the twin influences of Christianity and commerce, we have mostly gone beyond tribalism and into a more universalist state of mind.

Most people these days would be uncomfortable working magic which tried to force another person to act against their will. It's also generally discouraged to use magic that causes outright harm towards another person (though there is plenty of evidence that the ancients thought nothing of asking the Gods to curse their enemies!)

Various styles of magic were used, some of which remained in use down into the Dark Age and Medieval periods when the myths were being written down. One popular sort seems to have been chanted magic, and magic in the form of poetic verse. The spoken word was clearly regarded as having a great deal of power. There are accounts of Druids chanting over people whilst they went into trances.

More dramatic forms of magic involved calling up banks of fog to blind enemies, or raining down storms of fire.

Whether anyone ever actually did this, or it was simply the stuff of storytellers, we don't know. Visiting ravening thirsts on enemies, or preventing them from pissing, also seem to have been quite popular ways of temporarily disabling people.

The accounts of magical healing have been discussed in previous lessons, but stories range from herbal cures through to the re-attachment of severed limbs through chants and spells.

Shape-shifting has already been mentioned, and its importance cannot be emphasized enough. It forms the core of our approach to mysticism ~ transforming ones consciousness into something else, even if only for a short period, in order to learn something that will have a far greater effect later on. The goal of mysticism in some religions is to leave the physical world and its "distractions" behind, often with the implicit notion that the flesh is somehow corrupt and best eschewed. Such an approach sits ill with the passionate, life-embracing peoples described earlier. Far from rejecting the world, fath-fith seeks to embrace it in all its diversity, seeks to become bird or beast or tree.

In a related manner, to return to the story of the salmon, some forms of magic (such as the tarbh-feis ritual in which a sacrificed bull was eaten by a Druid who would then commune with its spirit) involve eating a source of magical power. The Druid aims to make the source part of her, either by shape-shifting into it, or by eating it. Some forms of spell involve dissolving barriers in order to unite with a magical force, let it become part of you whilst you (in turn) become part of it.

A useful image to bear in mind is that of a spider's web. The web is woven by the spider, which sits and waits for flies to land on the web. It senses the vibrations and acts accordingly. Our every action creates a strand of our personal web ~ each person we form a bond to, of love or hate, each place and object and idea we connect with builds up the network of the web. Everyone else is doing the same, so ultimately everything in the universe connects in some way or other to all the other webs. Clairvoyance can be thought of as rather like sensing a fly on the web, picking up on the emotions of someone to whom you are connected. Even the Gods are part of this, and weave their own exceedingly large webs as they go along.

Casting spells can be imagined as the deliberate attempt to weave our webs in a specific way ~ which is one of the reasons why so many spells require either the presence of the person to be effected, or some object linked with them. Where the link is weak, the spell will be ineffectual. The web, of course, is a two-way device. If you can sense and influence people to whom you are connected, then they can sense and influence you.

Of course, being a Druid doesn't make it compulsory that you have to cast three spells a fortnight. However, even if you have no interest in ever working magic yourself, it's a good idea to understand how it works and the ways other people might use it.

9.0 Druid Prophecy

The Druids ability to do prophecy is of great interest to me because I also have this ability and have had numerous prophetic experiences over the years. (See my book "Use Intuition and Prophecy to Improve Your Life"). This ability has always made me wonder if I have some Druidic ancestry.

A Picture of Modern Druidic Tarot Cards

They didn't have tarot cards (which came along in the 1400s), runes (those came later from the Anglo Saxons) or crystal balls (although those may have been in use as early as the year 500), but the Celts, and specifically the Druids, were big into divination – the art of seeing the future. Here are a few of the most common methods they used:

The Sight

Also called Second Sight, this is basic psychic ability. It was usually a trait of women and was thought to be passed in the female bloodline from mother to daughter. It was also developed among the prophetic class (Ovates) of

Druids. The visions seen and prophecy uttered by those with the sight, though often cryptic and filled with symbolism, were taken very seriously.

Forms of premonition, some of which we still joke about today, were also thought to tell the future in the body. Hence, if your mouth was itching, you'd soon be kissed, or if your ears were hot, someone was talking about your character.

Dreams

Sometimes a dream is just a dream, but sometimes it is much more. As a means of divination, they could come unsolicited, be expected, or even induced. Occasionally, their meaning was interpreted by Druid, but not as often as you'd think. If the dream was intentionally sought, the dreamer prepared by meditation, some kind of ritual purification (fasting was common) and animal sacrifice. In the case of the famous Bull Dream, the dreamer also slept in the hide of a sacred animal – a practice common to many shamanistic religions, including the Native Americans. (The Bull Dream was how the ancient kings of Tara in Ireland were selected.) In addition, some locations were thought to induce prophecy due to the presence of the supernatural, especially areas near water or sacred groves, so the location in which the dreamer slept could play an important role. Lastly, induced dreams were usually precipitated by the use of mind-altering herbs (something I don't recommend to anyone, just for the record), many of which are now considered poisonous.

Shoulder Blade Reading

We've all heard the tales of Druids reading entrails, but one distinctly Celtic form of divination is the reading of the marks in the shoulder blade of an animal, usually an ox, bear, fox or sheep. It was especially common in the Highlands of Scotland. This was an actual profession that consisted of boiling the bone, preparing it and reading the marks, which could indicate those people to be met in the future, while holes and indentations could mean death or prosperity depending on their size and location.

Omens

Omens were sought for nearly every activity, but were especially important when setting out on a journey. The first animal you saw, its posture and actions, as well as the gender, clothing and actions of the first person you meet on your way all foretold the success or failure of your quest. Birds were a special subset of animals known to foretell the future. Certain birds were sacred to the Celts and their flight patterns, calls and other behavior were used to divine the future. For the Irish, the raven and the wren were especially strong portents of the future.

Depending on the type of cry the bird gave and where it was positioned when it called, it could mean anything from the imminent arrival of visitors to death and doom for the household. (If you want details, read pages 144-146 of John Matthews's Secrets of the Druids. He gives an astonishing number of meanings.)

Casting Lots

Similar to the modern casting of ruins, the Celts would toss a group of sticks (some say made from the nine sacred woods), bones or stones and read the resulting pattern to see if a sick person would get well, to identify a future mate, or tell the positive or negative fortune of a person.

Everyday Divination

As mentioned in previous posts, there were also various other forms of common divination, usually to help find love, employed by the everyday Celts. These include the dancing of hazelnuts held over the fire at Samhain, the pattern in the ashes of the fire on Imbolc or dreaming of one's soul mate on Beltane. Scrying, or gazing into pools of water, flames of fire, or finding patterns in the clouds was also common among both Druids and everyday people.

10.0 Interesting Druid Facts and Stories

There is a lot more information about the Druids but and I thought an interesting way to end this book about them is to provide some interesting facts and legends:

Celtic Culture

The term "druid" applies to the religious figures within Celtic society. The Celts were an ancient people who were once spread out across western Europe but who are usually associated with Great Britain and Ireland

I Put a Spell on You!

While no genuinely Celtic sources survive from the Iron Age, Irish and Welsh sources did portray druids in their myths. These druids were often sorcerers or prophets predicting doom and gloom. They were also in very high positions of authority, which flew in the face of the Christian view of the older faiths.

Old-Timers

There is evidence that druids were practicing their religion as early as 25,000 years ago! Caves in France and Spain were covered in drawings of wild animals, and we also have ancient mounds and structures like Stonehenge thanks to the druids and their culture.

Written by the Victors

Most of our knowledge of Druidry (as it's often called) comes from historical documents written by the Ancient Romans, and later by the Christians. This puts historians in a bad spot, because the Celts and Romans were constantly at war with each other, and the Christians would absorb most of Celtic society. The Romans and Christians couldn't necessarily be trusted to give an unbiased account of the Celts, so we need to take their writing with a grain of salt.

Druid History, Mysticism, Rituals, Magic, and Prophecy

Try to Remember

The big reason why the druids didn't write about their own culture was because it was completely oral. Druids needed to know all their spells, rituals, and wisdom by heart. Julius Caesar wrote that druids could spend 20 years training for the job.

Smart Cookies

The druids—and the rest of the Celts—seem to have had a pretty advanced civilization back in the day. The existence of such stone circles as Stonehenge suggest that they were incredible builders. This means they would have had great engineering and mathematical skills. Unless, of course, you think Stonehenge was built by aliens or something like that.

Druid History, Mysticism, Rituals, Magic, and Prophecy

Know Your Place

The order of druids was divided into three sections. The Bards were charged with preserving the music and stories of their society. The Ovates practiced medicine, and also acted as clairvoyants. The Druids (with a capital D) were the philosophers and teachers, much like Aristotle and Plato were to their own society. They also acted as judges in time of need.

Under a Geas

Since the druids were often involved in foresight or prophecy, one of their powers could be the ability to invoke a geas upon someone. In the Irish mythologies, a geas was a rule, or spell, preventing someone from doing something at the risk of dying. This was seen as a blessing or a curse depending on the situation. Usually it was heroes affected by a geas who sometimes brought about their doom when they were forced to break their geas.

Taliesin

One famous example of a druid is Taliesin. According to what little we know of Taliesin, he was a famous bard who sang for at least three British kings. As the years went on, he's become a legendary figure associated with Bran the Blessed, and even King Arthur.

The Gods Want Blood

When they wrote about the Celts, the Romans often commented on their rituals of human sacrifice to the gods. There is room for argument on the subject, but allegedly, the druids would be responsible for sacrificing to different gods in different ways. One god wanted men to be hanged, while another insisted on drowning them.

Sometimes prisoners and criminals were used, but it's been suspected that some sacrifices died willingly.

Big Fans of Arbor Day

One thing that defined the Celtic religion was the sacred grove. A grove is a cluster of trees, and the druids would fence off certain groves for their rituals. Even the basis of their name (as we discussed earlier) indicates how important trees were to Druidry.

Imbas Forosnai

In ancient Ireland, there was the tradition of *Imbas forosnai*, which was the gift of clairvoyance. It was supposedly practiced by the great poets of Celtic Ireland. For the Celts, spiritual truth was usually conveyed through poetry.

Die Hard 3

One of the more hardcore beliefs of the druids was the threefold death. In one version of the threefold death, an individual has three simultaneous causes of death; for example, wounding, hanging, and drowning. These causes of death were usually a punishment predicted in advance, and naturally there's only a few recorded instances of them, given how unlikely a triple death happens in life.

They Always Come in Threes

The number three was very important to Druidry. Aside from the threefold death and the three classes of druids, there was a belief in Gaul that the universe was divided into three parts. The Celts had also adopted the ancient symbol of three conjoined spirals, known as the triskelion.

British Bias

When the Romans first invaded Britain under Caesar's command, they made a lot of discoveries about how the Britons lived and what Britain was like. Caesar himself speculated that Britain was where Druidism first came from, and it was brought to mainland Europe from there.

Sacred Island

In Britain, one location sacred to the druids is the island of Ynys Mon, also known as Anglesey. Historical documents go out of their way to point this out, looking at Ynys Mon like it's a sort of enemy base. It was noted for its collection of sacred groves and monuments.

The Oak & Mistletoe Ritual

According to noted Roman historian Pliny the Elder, the druids had a ritual for the moment when rare mistletoe was discovered growing on an oak branch. This was the spiritual jackpot for the Celts, so the druids would sacrifice two white bulls while cutting down the mistletoe with a golden sickle. The mistletoe was said to be an antidote to poison. Pliny's passage has gone on to influence much of how we view druids to this day.

May Day Holiday

In Wales, the druids and the rest of the Celts celebrated Calan Mai on the first day of May. It was seen as the midpoint between summer and winter, so the two seasons would have a fight that was acted out by the people. It was also seen as a day for divination and contacting the dead. The tradition of lighting bonfires was preserved in Wales long after Druidry had been wiped out.

Stephen King, Eat Your Heart Out

Once again proving that the Irish had the best kind of mythology, a power that was often associated with the druids was known as the féth fíada. This referred to an enchanted mist that druids would use to hide themselves from their enemies in times of need. Naturally, this awesome bit of mythology was later stolen and went on to be associated with early Christian saints.

Afterlife

Druidry has a few different ideas of the Otherworld, but its general idea remains the same across the board. After death, people went to the Otherworld, a place that is associated with joy and celebration. Warriors feast together, people are forever young, and time is no longer a thing. Mythological heroes were able to visit the Otherworld and return to the land of the living, and some believed that the dead would eventually be reincarnated.

Those Bloody Romans

The Romans hated the Celts, and Julius Caesar made a career out of conquering Gaul. Subsequent emperors waged a war on the druids, trying to stamp out their religions in favor of the Roman ones. Augustus allegedly made it illegal for druids to be Roman citizens.

Island Massacre

Britain took a little longer for the Romans to subdue, so the Romans made sure to hit them where it hurt. Tacitus proudly describes the terrifying invasion of Ynys Mon by Suetonius Paulinus, the slaughter of the druids, and the destruction of the groves.

Christians Move In

Eventually the Romans converted to Christianity, a religion that stuck around even after the Roman Empire disappeared. Christianity completed the destruction of old Druidry, as they were reduced to being midwives and village healers. For their part, the Christians plundered Druidry and adopted many things for their own faith.

We'll Take That Word Too!

The druids worshipped the seasonal solstices and equinoxes as part of the idea that life is a series of renewing cycles. Their word for winter solstice was "Yule," which people might realize is the same name of a tradition stolen by the Christians to enhance Christmas.

Irish Hero

Saint Patrick, that honored saint of Ireland who turned it Christian, was noted by writers for challenging, and ultimately overthrowing, the order of druids in Ireland. Murchiú's writing even gives the druids a prophecy where they predict Patrick's arrival and triumph. In it, he's depicted as being crazy, which is an attempt to show how much Patrick was hated by his enemies.

Bring Back the Past

Ancient Celtic religions had been all but wiped out during the first thousand years of Christianity dominating the post-Roman world. By the 1700s, however, some people had begun to look back and help bring about a sort of revival for Druidism. These people included artist and poet William Blake!

So Why the Change of Heart?

There are a few reasons why Druidism was brought back from near extinction. It was around this time that the age of exploration exposed people to the Aboriginal tribes of the

Americas. While most called them savages, some admired these people for their closeness with nature and their spiritual peace despite never being near Christianity. Also, ancient texts were being translated, and gave people a whole new slate of sources on their Celtic ancestors, and this led to some serious nostalgia.

Struggle for the Stones

Stonehenge remains the most famous place of worship to Druidry for both old and new practitioners. In 1905, a gathering of nearly 300 neo-druids held a ceremony at Stonehenge, even as the newspapers back then mocked the group.

Respect Your Elders

Modern Druids believe in a connection to their ancestors and show them proper respect. This has led to neo-druids leading campaigns to re-bury skeletons being held in museums or science labs. The scientific community has responded with arguments of their own.

The Druidry Dos and Don'ts

Neo-druidry has no universal instructions on ritual, but they're most often performed outside when the sun is at its peak in the sky. The group stands in a circle and calls to the four winds while ceremonial food and drink is passed around. Energy from the earth is then summoned during a period of meditation. This usually concludes, in the time-honored British fashion, with a visit to the local pub.

We Invented Halloween

One of the origins of Halloween is the sacred day of Samhain. This was the last harvest day, but also an eerie, spiritual day. The druids declared that on Samhain, the living and the dead were closest to each other than on any other day. So of course, the Christians eventually adopted it into a day of fear and spooky ghosts that only pagans would find meaningful.

The Dead Marshes

Throughout the years, bodies have been found preserved within peat bogs, giving rise to the term "bog bodies." While this would cause most people to never set foot in the bogs ever again, archaeologists continue to make discoveries. Many corpses date back to the Iron Age, the best example being Old Croghan Man. Based on the evidence we've discovered about his life and death, a popular theory is that he was a human sacrifice to one of the many Celtic gods whom the druids would worship.

Still Sounds Better Than Burning Man

Julius Caesar himself wrote of the rituals of human sacrifice that he witnessed among the druids, the most frightening of which was the legendary wicker man. He said that the druids would build an enormous, wooden effigy of a man and place sacrifices inside (ideally criminals who had been sentenced to death, but slaves would do in a pinch). The wooden idol would then be set on fire, and the people inside would be burned alive. This image paints a particularly gruesome image of the druids, but it is important to remember that Caesar spent his life fighting Gaelic peoples, and so his opinion may not be the most credible

11.0 Summary

As you can see from the materials in this book on the Druids that they were ancient priests, prophets, healers, and leaders of an early Celtic culture.

It is hard to learn about the Druids because they didn't write any of their knowledge down.

The Tuatha Da Dannan are said to have originally come from the Otherworld. I find it really interesting that according to mythical histories the Tuatha Da Dannan they were the ancestors of the Druids, Elves, and Leprechauns among others.

The Druids also seem to have developed the precursors of modern witchcraft practices.

I love learning that the Druids also had prophecy as a big part of their practices since I have had many prophecy experiences of my own.

All the Best,

Martin K. Ettington
2022

12.0 Bibliography

1. https://www.historic-uk.com/HistoryUK/HistoryofWales/Druids/. *Druids.* [Online]

2. https://druidnetwork.org/what-is-druidry/learning-resources/polytheist/lesson-seventeen/. *Druids and Magic.* [Online]

3. https://druidnetwork.org/what-is-druidry/learning-resources/. *learning Resources.* [Online]

4. https://www.ancient-origins.net/myths-legends-europe/legendary-origins-merlin-magician-002627. *Legendary Origins of Merlin the Magician.* [Online]

5. https://www.ladyofthelakeherbs.com/druid-herbs.html. *Druid Herbs.* [Online]

6. https://druidry.org/druid-way/teaching-and-practice/druid-festivals/the-eightfold-wheel-of-the-year. *The Eightfold Wheel of the Year.* [Online]

7. https://www.factinate.com/things/44-occult-facts-druids/. *44 Occult Facts Druids.* [Online]

8. https://nicoleevelina.com/2012/06/21/i-is-for-insight-celtic-divination/. *Insight into Celtic Divination.* [Online]

9. https://druidry.org/druid-way/teaching-and-practice/meditation/tree-meditation. *Tree Meditation.* [Online] 2023.

10. https://druidnetwork.org/what-is-druidry/learning-resources/garden-meditation/. *Garden Meditation.* [Online] 2008.

11. https://darachcroft.com/news/the-gaelic-tree-alphabet. *The Gaelic Tree Al[phabet.* [Online]

Druid History, Mysticism, Rituals, Magic, and Prophecy

13.0 Index

Druid History, Mysticism, Rituals, Magic, and Prophecy